Pensions and Productivity

Stuart Dorsey
Christopher Cornwell
David Macpherson

1998

W.E. Upjohn Institute for Employment Research
Kalamazoo, Michigan

Library of Congress Cataloging-in-Publication Data

Dorsey, Stuart.
  Pensions and productivity / Stuart Dorsey, Christopher Cornwell,
David Macpherson.
    p. cm.
  Includes bibliographical references and index.
  ISBN 0–88099–186–0 (alk. paper). — ISBN 0–88099–185–2
(pbk. : alk. paper)
  1. Pensions. 2. Old age pensions. 3. Pension trusts. 4. Early
retirement incentives. 5. Labor productivity. I. Cornwell,
Christopher Mark. II. Macpherson, David A., 1960– . III. Title.
HD7105.3.D67 1998
331.25'2—dc21   98–17997
                                                                                      CIP

Copyright © 1998
W. E. Upjohn Institute for Employment Research
300 S. Westnedge Avenue
Kalamazoo, Michigan 49007–4686

Cover design by J. R. Underhill
Index prepared by Leoni Z. McVey.
Printed in the United States of America.

CONTENTS

LIST OF TABLES

LIST OF FIGURES

Acknowledgments

The authors thank Richard Ippolito, William Even, Steven Woodbury, Allan Hunt, and Jean Kimmel for carefully reviewing this monograph and providing helpful suggestions. We also appreciate the comments of participants at seminars at Miami University, the Federal Reserve Bank of Cleveland, and the W.E. Upjohn Institute.

The Authors

Stuart Dorsey is Professor of Economics and Vice-President and Academic Dean at Baker University. He was previously an Associate Professor of Economics at West Virginia University, staff economist for the U.S. Senate Finance Committee, and economist at the Pension and Welfare Benefits Office of the U.S. Department of Labor. His primary research interest is pensions and labor market incentives. Dorsey holds a Ph.D. in economics from Washington University (St. Louis, Missouri).

Christopher Cornwell is an Associate Professor of Economics at the University of Georgia. He has been a visiting professor at the Universitaet Erlangen-Nuernberg (Nuernberg, Germany), Monash University (Melbourne, Australia), and Universite Jean Moulin (Lyon, France), as well as a visiting scholar at the Federal Reserve Bank of Cleveland. His research is concentrated in the areas of applied econometrics and productivity measurement. Cornwell received his Ph.D. in economics from Michigan State University.

David Macpherson is Professor of Economics and Research Director of the Pepper Institute on Aging and Public Policy at Florida State University. His specialty is applied labor economics. His current research interests include pensions, discrimination, industry deregulation, labor unions, and the minimum wage. He is co-author of the annual *Union Membership and Earnings Data Book: Compilations from the Current Population Survey*, published by the Bureau of National Affairs. He is also a co-author of the undergraduate labor economics text *Contemporary Labor Economics*. He received his Ph.D. from Pennsylvania State University in 1987.

1 Pensions and the Labor Market

INTRODUCTION

The study of internal labor markets, also known as "the new economics of personnel," has made important contributions to labor economics. This research has attempted to explain policies governing employee-employer relationships when the job match is productive and durable, addressing such questions as, What is the economic basis for durable employment relationships? How can compensation and promotion policies provide incentives to attract and motivate quality employees? When job matches are productive, how can wages and benefits simultaneously allocate productivity gains and discourage quits and layoffs?

Internal labor market research is in the spirit of the "new institutional economics" (Simon 1991), in that a frequent theme is modeling labor market practices and policies as efficient and productivity-enhancing solutions to the incentive problems that arise from asymmetric or incomplete information. Economists have applied this approach to wage and employment factors such as earnings that rise with tenure, interindustry wage differentials, promotions and bonuses, and incentives for early retirement.[1]

Pensions are one of the most important workplace institutions. Nearly half of all private-sector employees participate in a retirement plan, and pension costs are approximately 5 percent of payroll for the sponsoring firms (U.S. Chamber of Commerce 1994). Most studies of private pensions have focused on the advantages of saving for retirement through a pension. Pensions provide a large and growing share of income for retirees: 44 percent of all households with persons above age 65 received pension income in 1994 (Grad 1996), and this figure is estimated to rise to 76 percent by 2018 (Silverman and Yakoboski 1994). Private pension plans paid $179.4 billion in benefits in 1994 (EBRI 1997), almost one-third of total retirement payments, and provided 9 percent of total income for the elderly (Grad 1996).

The internal labor market perspective suggests that pensions, in addition to providing a vehicle for retirement saving, establish incentives that promote productivity. The defined-benefit plan—which, despite recent trends to greater defined-contribution coverage, is still the dominant form of coverage—typically rewards long tenure and penalizes late retirement. Employees covered by a defined-benefit plan maximize their pension wealth by working without breaks in tenure until they reach retirement age. A pension loss is incurred by leaving either "too early" or "too late." Defined-contribution pensions, by their construction, are more neutral towards quit or retirement decisions.[2]

This monograph applies the internal labor market perspective to private pension incentives. The popularity of defined-benefit coverage—well over half of the workers with pensions still are covered by these plans—argues that pension incentives have important economic functions. Because private pensions are voluntary, and given the availability of defined-contribution plans that offer a simpler, lower-cost retirement savings vehicle, defined-benefit plans must convey distinct advantages. The internal labor market perspective suggests that one of the advantages is incentives for higher productivity.

PERSPECTIVES ON PENSIONS

Demand-Side

Why do employers compensate their employees with pensions? A large body of research has explored both demand- and supply-oriented theories of pension coverage.[3] Demand-side theories start from the proposition that employers are indifferent between paying cash wages or making contributions to a pension fund, and thus pensions are sponsored to satisfy employee demand for a retirement saving vehicle. A reduction in income taxes is a well-known reason for employees to prefer pension saving. Employer contributions and the interest and dividend earnings of pension assets are not taxed until benefits are paid. Therefore, compensating workers by credibly promising future pension benefits, rather than the equivalent value of cash wages, can yield important tax savings, especially for high-income employees. There is much empirical evidence that pension coverage responds to tax incentives.[4]

Another demand-side theory is that pensions are an insurance policy against a number of retirement-age risks. One such risk is that retirees will live longer than expected and their savings will be depleted before death. The market solution to this risk is an annuity, which pays a fixed sum as long as the individual is alive. Adverse selection problems arise, however, when annuities are purchased late in life, because older persons in poor health will refuse to purchase annuities. Pensions solve this problem by requiring workers to, in effect, purchase a retirement annuity when they accept a job and begin participating in the plan. At this younger age, differences in expected lifespans are less evident.

A third reason why workers prefer pension saving is to shift the risk of poor investment performance to the employer. The employer appears to assume the risk of adverse asset performance in a defined-benefit plan by promising a retirement benefit based upon the worker's earnings, rather than the value of the pension fund. If future earnings are less variable than asset prices, employees enjoy greater certainty about retirement living standards under defined-benefit plans.[5]

Other demand-centered pension theories are that economies of scale in administering private pensions allow workers to earn higher rates of return, net of expenses, by group retirement saving (Mitchell and Andrews 1981); and that unions prefer pensions because they disproportionately benefit members with greater seniority (Freeman 1985). Evidence that pension coverage, especially through defined-benefit plans, is more likely in large, unionized establishments supports these theories (Dorsey 1987, for example).

While there are many demand-side theories of defined-benefit plans, most defined-contribution plans are consistent only with tax savings.[6] These plans create a retirement account to which the employer or employee make regular contributions. Benefits are based upon the value of the assets in the account at retirement, unlike defined-benefit plans, which pay an annuity based upon age, earnings, or years of service. Retirees also may elect a lump-sum benefit, unlike most defined-benefit participants.

Yet, demand-side theories do not address the incentives created by pensions, particularly by defined-benefit plans. The tax savings aspect could be exploited with the administratively simpler defined-contribution plan, and defined-benefit plans could shift risk to employers, with age- and earnings-based annuities, without imposing quit or late retirement penalties.

Supply-Side

A supply-side perspective is that pension incentives raise workforce productivity and lower labor costs. Internal labor market theories suggest several mechanisms through which pensions promote productivity. The nonportability of defined-benefit pension wealth penalizes quits, an incentive which may promote investments in employee training. The threat of loss of pension benefits also may discourage shirking and lower the cost of monitoring employee effort. Pensions, whether defined-benefit or defined-contribution, are valued more by workers who have low internal discount rates. Many have suggested that such forward-looking persons are more productive long-term employees.[7] In addition, defined-benefit plans are a convenient vehicle for rewarding early retirement. With mandatory retirement rules no longer legal, pension bonuses are perhaps the only feasible way to encourage the early exit of older workers, whose productivity may have declined or become more variable.

An alternative supply-side perspective is based on the ability to underfund defined-benefit pensions. Underfunding, by definition impossible in defined-contribution plans, converts employees into unsecured bondholders. Ippolito (1986) has argued that this creates an incentive for group productivity gains, particularly in union settings. Some financial economists see underfunding as a less expensive source of financing than borrowing from outsiders, given imperfect information in credit markets.[8]

The supply-side view that pensions enhance productivity is primarily a theory of defined-benefit plans, because of the latter's ease of establishing incentives for tenure and retirement. Defined-contribution plans, however, also can attract workers who have low discount rates. Recent empirical pension studies suggest that defined-contribution plans also promote favorable labor market outcomes, such as reduced quits.

SIGNIFICANCE OF THE PRODUCTIVITY THEORY
OF PENSIONS

Economic studies of pensions frequently assume that defined-benefit pensions raise productivity.[9] This supply-side view follows from the economist's presumption that pension incentives must create value sufficient to offset their costs. Constraints on workers' ability to move to more attractive jobs or to retire when they wish are costly, requiring employers to pay compensating wage premiums to attract workers. In firms where pension incentives serve no productive function, employers could attract workers at a lower cost by offering defined-contribution pensions. Alternatively, sponsors could write plan rules to increase benefit portability and to eliminate late retirement penalties. This reasoning implies that defined-benefit pensions are part of a compensation package in jobs where long tenure or early retirement is productive.

In contrast, outside the economics literature, the possibility that pensions may be a tool to enhance productivity is ignored or explicitly discounted in much of the discussion of pensions and pension policy. The human resource management perspective almost exclusively sees pensions as driven by employee preferences. For example, we reviewed several current human resource management college textbooks and found little discussion of the implications of different pension plan types for turnover or retirement decisions. Some texts failed even to describe the implications of the different incentive structures of defined-benefit and defined-contribution plans.[10] No book that we reviewed integrated pensions into discussions of designing strategic compensation systems.[11] The imperfect portability of benefits generally was presented as a disadvantage of defined-benefit plans, rather than as an intentional compensation policy. Pensions generally were discussed in the context of employee benefits, with attention strictly on providing for employees' retirement security, and nonportable benefits can lower pension wealth. This is a perspective in which pensions are exclusively a vehicle for providing retirement income.

The human resource management professional literature also is largely silent on the possible advantages of pension incentives. One of the authors searched the human resource professional journals and found little research on the effect of pension plan choices on employee outcomes or performance (Dorsey 1995). Issues of equity and adequacy of replacement rates dominated the discussion of pension plan design. Again, nonportability was treated as a shortcoming of defined-benefit plans.[12]

Human resource professionals also assign little value to pension tenure incentives. Most, however, appreciate the ability of defined-benefit plans to encourage early retirement. The following statement by Marc W. Twinney, an administrator of a large pension fund, is fairly representative of the opinions of benefit professionals:

> The primary reason larger, international manufacturing firms provide private pensions is to remove the older, less efficient employee from the work force in a socially responsible way. Firms do not provide pensions to recruit. . . . (or) to tie employees to the work force and avoid recruiting or training costs. The fact that this occurs is incidental to the primary goal. These secondary effects result from controlling the costs of providing retirement income and are acceptable to the firm and its employees. (Schmitt 1993, p. 98.)

Lazear (1990) also concluded that benefit managers primarily understand pensions as retirement savings vehicles, suggesting that they frequently fail even to understand the implications of pension incentives on work force outcomes, let alone see them as having strategic value.

Economics is about incentives, so it is not surprising that economists are more likely to think about why pension tenure and retirement incentives might be useful to firms and workers. Even the economics literature, however, often has characterized pension quit penalties as impediments to efficient job mobility. Turner (1993) describes two arguments for legislation to enhance pension portability. First, greater portability will raise retirement benefits of workers who, for whatever reason, have experienced frequent or untimely job changes. Second, reduced quits induced by nonportability lowers productivity by tying workers to jobs where their productivity has fallen due to shifts in consumer tastes or technology shocks.

The latter concern, popularly known as "job lock," has been around for some time. Ross (1958) labeled it the "new industrial feudalism." Choate and Linger (1986, p. 245) wrote, "Weaknesses in pension availability, benefits, and portability are now impeding the mobility that is so essential during this period of economic and technological turbulence, as an aging work force avoids job changes to protect pension rights." The claim that nonportability restricts productive job changes implies that pensions are motivated by tax and insurance functions and that incentives for long tenure are perhaps an historical accident based upon early optimistic assessments of their beneficial effects and preserved by institutional rigidity.

The productive value of pension incentives is an important issue in the economics of pensions and for evaluating pension policy. Consider the debate over pension portability policy. For the past 20 years, the United States and Canada have moved toward increasing retirement benefit portability. In the United States, the minimum vesting period has been lowered twice since 1975 and currently stands at five years. Most Canadian provinces now require vesting in defined-benefit plans after two years. In addition to mandating greater portability in defined-benefit plans, changes in tax and regulatory policy in the United States have increased the attractiveness of defined-contribution plans (Clark and McDermed 1990), which are by definition more portable.[13] Pension reform advocates continue to argue for higher portability standards for defined-benefit pensions. Mandatory portability may raise the value of workers' pension wealth[14] and promote job mobility. If pension incentives promote long tenure where the latter is productive, however, greater portability will have a cost.

An understanding of the productivity view of pensions also is needed to interpret and evaluate coverage trends. Primary coverage by defined-benefit plans declined from 87 percent of participants in 1975 to 57 percent in 1993. While the defined-benefit coverage remains important, the shift raises important questions. Do plan sponsors believe that pension incentives are less important today, i.e., have the productivity gains from defined-benefit plans diminished? Or do rising costs of administering these plans, fueled by federal regulations, explain much of the trend? If the latter, does the substitution of defined-contribution coverage imply weaker employee/firm attachment and lower productivity? Will this trend continue, with defined-benefit plans eventually becoming obsolete?

Finally, a clearer understanding of the importance of pension incentives provides a stronger foundation for future pension research. This monograph will review labor market models which feature long-term employment and will survey previous empirical pension studies. An important outcome will be suggestions for future research. We will present some new empirical results; however, extensive testing of the productivity theory of pensions will require a major investment in data collection.

ORGANIZATION OF THIS DISCUSSION

Our analysis of the productivity theory of pensions is in three parts. First, we review the history and institutional practices of private pensions and government policy towards pensions. Chapter 2 traces the origins of private pensions in the United States and the evolution of current coverage. Tax rules and regulations have had a major impact on pensions, and this chapter concludes with an overview of federal policies. Chapter 3 describes institutional pension practices which create incentives. We show how workers who leave a job that has a defined-benefit pension are penalized. The advantages of defined-benefit plans in establishing retirement incentives also are presented. We also discuss more recent ideas about how defined-contribution plans may convey productive incentives.

Second, we consider whether pension incentives are consistent with models of internal labor markets. Chapter 4 reviews employment models in which specific training and monitoring costs generate job-specific productivity gains. Mechanisms to discourage early quitting or late retirement are needed to enforce long-term employment contracts. We compare pension incentives with ideal solutions.

Third, we evaluate empirical evidence that pensions promote productivity. Chapter 5 reviews empirical studies which test the pension-productivity hypothesis. We find little direct evidence that pensions enhance productivity, but a number of studies provide indirect evidence consistent with the hypothesis. This chapter also takes up the question of the growing popularity of defined-contribution plans and considers whether the declining market share of defined-benefit plans is evidence that pension incentives are no longer important.

The next two chapters report new empirical evidence. Chapter 6 tests a channel through which pensions may enhance worker productivity: by promoting investments in worker training. We created a new data set by matching Current Population Surveys, allowing us to test the prediction of the specific-training model that pensions and training are complements. Chapter 7 reports direct estimates of productivity gains for firms that sponsor defined-benefit pensions. We estimate parameters of a production function using firm data from the Compustat file. These are pieces of evidence which advance the empirical literature, but significant data and modeling issues will remain.

We will disappoint readers looking for a single, definitive test of the productivity theory versus other pension theories. The ideal empirical study would be based on a structural model of pension coverage, labor force outcomes, and productivity (Figure 1.1). Such a model would recognize that pension coverage is endogenous and would test the importance of productivity factors against demand-side theories of why firms sponsor pensions. It simultaneously would estimate the channels through which pension incentives raised productivity, as suggested by long-term employment models: e.g., by encouraging employee training. Finally, it would link improved labor force outcomes to productivity gains. No data set exists which will support such a powerful test.[15] This should not be too surprising, given that such a data set would allow tests of more basic and direct incentives, such as wage policies, that also have eluded economists.

Although our goals are less ambitious than estimating a fully specified structural model, they are still important: to analyze and explain thoroughly the channels through which pensions may promote productivity; to summarize the existing literature; to advance the empirical literature with new results; and to help frame future empirical work.

Figure 1.1 A Unified Pension Model

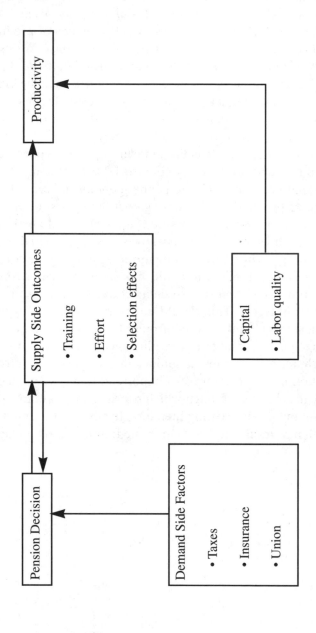

NOTES

1. An excellent discussion of applying competitive market solutions to internal labor market problems of imperfect information and moral hazard is found in Lazear (1991). Carmichael (1989) provides a concise discussion of implicit labor contracts. Another fine nontechnical discussion of the internal labor market perspective is Wachter and Wright (1990).

2. After workers are vested, quit costs are zero in most defined-contribution plans. While it may be possible to increase contribution rates with age and tenure, the tax advantages of deferring compensation under defined-benefit plans are large compared with backloaded contributions or deferred wages. The reasons why defined-benefit plans are a superior vehicle for establishing tenure and retirement incentives are explored in Chapter 3.

3. For surveys of this literature, see Bodie (1990) and Gustman, Mitchell, and Steinmeier (1994).

4. Cross-section analyses show a large positive effect of income on pension coverage (Dorsey 1982). Alpert (1983), Woodbury and Huang (1991), and Reagan and Turner (1994) report that the likelihood of coverage rises with marginal tax rates.

5. Pesando and Hyatt (1992), however, point out that defined-benefit plans do not necessarily shield employees from investment risk. They present evidence that when lower investment earnings require higher pension contributions, employers reduce wage increases or other benefits. There also is direct evidence that ad hoc inflation adjustments are more likely when pension fund returns are high (Allen, Clark, and McDermed 1992), causing real pension benefits to fall when unexpected inflation lowers asset returns.

6. Defined-contribution plans in theory could prohibit lump-sum distributions. In practice, 96 percent of defined-contribution beneficiaries in 1989 received at least a portion of their benefits as a lump-sum distribution (Turner and Beller 1992).

7. See Ippolito (1998). There is a large body of research in the field of psychology which indicates that individuals who are able to delay gratification achieve higher levels of success (Mischel, Shoda, and Rodriguez 1989).

8. Of course, the reduction in financing costs must be sufficient to offset the tax losses when the firm's real pension obligations are underfunded.

9. These studies include, for example, Rice (1966), Blinder (1982), Long and Scott (1982), Ippolito (1986), Allen and Clark (1987), Even and Macpherson (1996), and Curme and Even (1995).

10. The most detailed presentations of pension incentives was found in Miner and Crane (1995).

11. An exception was Noe et al. (1994), who wrote that "The typical pension is *designed* to discourage employee turnover" (p. 644, our emphasis). They also note the importance of pensions as severance payments for firms that are reducing the size of their workforce. To provide some perspective, these texts also place less emphasis than labor economics on the incentive functions of wages and compensation policies in general. For example, there also was little mention of

deferred wages or efficiency wages in chapters on turnover or strategic compensation.

12. For example, Brennan (1984), in an article on restructuring corporate pension plans, recommended switching to a career-average benefit formula to enhance the portability of the defined-benefit plan.

13. These trends have been less evident in Canada; however, recent policy changes have caused concern that defined-benefit plans may begin to lose popularity there as well.

14. Employers may respond to portability requirements by lowering the generosity of pensions. Thus, legislation may have no effect on pension wealth or costs.

15. Gustman and Mitchell (1992) present a detailed discussion of the data needed to test a structural model of pension coverage. Data that are currently available fall well short of these requirements.

2 An Overview
of Private Pensions and Policy

This chapter briefly describes essential characteristics of the private pension system in the United States and the federal tax and regulatory policies that have affected pensions.[1] The concept that pensions could raise productivity and lower labor costs is hardly new. The first industrial plans were conceived as a human resource management tool. Ironically (given the current lack of interest by managers), economic historians have concluded that facilitating early retirement and reducing turnover were the primary stimuli to the first wave of pension adoptions in the early twentieth century.

Industrial pensions became widespread just after the turn of the century among large employers in railroads, utilities, banking, and manufacturing. According to Williamson (1994) and Graebner (1980), firms that sponsored pensions before 1910 were primarily motivated by retirement concerns. Interest in pensions had grown in the late nineteenth century as the idea became widespread that older workers were less productive, or even unsafe to fellow employees or customers. Older employees generally were perceived as unable to adapt to the new, more rigid and physically demanding technologies that were spreading across industry at the turn of the century.[2] The traditional practice of providing older workers continued employment with reduced responsibilities was costly. Yet employers wanted to be perceived as treating older workers fairly in order to maintain the morale and loyalty of younger employees. Employers hoped that adopting mandatory retirement, complemented by a pension, would enhance productivity, safety, and promotion opportunities for younger workers.

An excellent example is the introduction of the first modern pension by the Pennsylvania Railroad, described by Gratton (1990). The Pennsylvania Railroad, one of the largest employers in the country, instituted a universal, noncontributory pension in 1900. At the same time, workers were required to retire at age 70, and the company also adopted an explicit policy of not hiring new employees older than age 35. Gratton cites persuasive evidence that the railroad's policy was driven by a perceived opportunity to cut labor costs by eliminating older employees from the workforce. Company analysts had estimated that older workers were one-third less productive, on average, yet were paid one-third more than new hires.

Early pension adopters also were concerned about high turnover, which had reached extraordinary levels in manufacturing industries. By 1910, hiring and training costs had grown dramatically. Turnover rates of 200 percent were not uncommon in manufacturing firms, and the turnover rate at Ford Motor Company in Detroit reached 370 percent in 1911 (Slichter 1921).

The "scientific management" philosophy gained momentum during this period, spurring pension adoptions. This approach, sometimes known as "Taylorism" for its chief proponent, Dr. Frederick Taylor, emphasized worker productivity through measurement and explicit incentives. In this management environment, pensions were seen as raising productivity by reducing turnover. Nonvested, defined-benefit pensions spread quickly among large firms in the United States and Canada between 1910 and 1930, and Latimer (1932) attributed much of this growth to the turnover problem.[3]

Graebner (1980, p. 129) reached a similar conclusion, citing the example of DuPont Corporation: "Turnover was clearly the dominant consideration in DuPont deliberations over a new pension plan in 1914." A review of internal memoranda revealed that key DuPont officials believed that a retirement plan would mitigate the company's high turnover rate.[4] DuPont officials also favored early vesting in order to make the program attractive to younger workers.

Graebner (p. 128) quotes a banker friend of Coleman DuPont, who advised quick adoption of a pension: "The right sort of pension plan comes pretty near being a panacea for most of the ills that exist between employer and employee . . . there is hardly any workforce problem facing management today that cannot be solved by the adoption of a pension plan."

Other factors, of course, may have contributed to the spread of pensions. Some writers have suggested that an unfunded, unvested pension discouraged union organization; or that firms were concerned for the welfare of older employees who had grown physically unable to work, consistent with the view of pensions as retirement income insurance. We could not find any historical evidence, however, suggesting that establishing a source of "insider" financing was a factor in early pension growth. Early pension adoptions appear to have been driven by the concerns of personnel offices.

Optimism about the beneficial effects of pensions was short-lived. Latimer (1932) reported that by the end of the 1920s, few managers had confidence that pensions did much to lower turnover. He argued that, by the late 1920s, the principal economic justification for pensions had evolved into enabling mandatory retirement, a view that remains popular with human resource professionals.

Pension coverage grew slowly in industries other than railroads, utilities, banking, and manufacturing, and by 1940 the great majority of private sector workers still had no private retirement plan. Private sector coverage began a steady climb during World War II, however, reaching a peak of 45 percent in 1970 (Table 2.1), and 43 percent of total private sector workers now are covered under an employer-sponsored pension plan. There is evidence that coverage rates may have declined slightly since the mid 1970s.[5] The stability of the aggregate rates, however, masks a very large decline in coverage for young males (Even and Macpherson 1994), while women's coverage rates have risen significantly.

While defined-benefit coverage has declined steadily and substantially since 1975, over half of all workers with pensions still have primary coverage under this type of pension (Table 2.2). Defined-benefit plans promise workers a retirement annuity based upon years of service and, usually, the worker's highest earnings. Internal Revenue Service rules generally prohibit pre-tax employee contributions to a pension fund, and most defined-benefit plans do not require employee contributions. Since the employee's pension wealth is in the form of a promised benefit, defined-benefit plans have rules which specify participation, vesting, and benefit eligibility.

Federal law requires that full-time employees who are at least age 21 with one year of service be allowed to participate, i.e., begin earning service credit. Pension vesting rules define the portion of a worker's accrued benefit that he or she owns upon leaving the firm. Before federal regulations were implemented in 1975, nearly half of defined-benefit plans had no provision for vesting separated employees; i.e., workers who left before retirement lost all pension benefits (Kolodrubetz and Landay 1973). The Employee Retirement Income Security Act (ERISA) required plans to vest employees under a graduated

Table 2.1 Private Sector Pension Coverage

Year	Private sector workers covered (%)	Full-time private sector workers covered (%)
1940	15	17
1945	19	21
1950	25	29
1955	32	37
1960	41	47
1965	43	49
1970	45	52
1979	43	50
1983	41	47
1988	42	48
1993	43	

SOURCE: Estimates for 1940–70 were calculated by Beller and Lawrence (1992) and include only nonagricultural workers. Estimates for 1979–93 are calculated from pension supplements to the Current Population Survey and do not exclude agricultural employees.

Table 2.2 Trends in Pension Plan Type

Year	Defined-benefit plans (% of all plans)	Participating workers with primary defined-benefit coverage (%)
1975	33	87
1977	30	85
1979	30	83
1981	31	81
1983	29	77
1985	27	73
1987	22	67
1989	18	64
1990	16	62
1991	15	62
1992	13	57
1993	12	56

SOURCE: U.S. Department of Labor, *Private Pension Plan Bulletin (1997)*. Calculations are based on Internal Revenue Service Form 5500 reports.

schedule or a "cliff" rule. Most plans chose the latter, under which employees' legal entitlement jumped from zero to 100 percent of formula benefits at 10 years of service. The legal standard for a single-employer plan was raised to five-year cliff or seven-year graded vesting by the Tax Reform Act of 1986.[6] These regulations have contributed to a higher vesting rate. Sixty-six percent of active participants were fully vested by 1993, compared with 36 percent in 1975 (U.S. Department of Labor 1997).

Most covered workers must satisfy age and service minimums before they begin to receive benefits. The sole criterion is age in 43 percent of defined-benefit plans, and among these 65 years is the most common standard. The remainder use either a minimum years of service plus age (e.g., 85 years) or have both age and service minimums. A common combined requirement is age 62 plus 10 years of service. Thus, many employees are eligible to retire with full benefits before reaching age 65.

Almost all defined benefit plans provide for early retirement with reduced benefits. Two-thirds of participants are eligible for a reduced benefit at age 55 if they have met service requirements (generally, 10 or 15 years). Also, a growing number of plans permit retirement before age 65 with unreduced benefits.[7]

Prior to 1986, over half of defined-benefit plans gave no service credit for years that employees worked past age 65. The Omnibus Budget Reconciliation Act of 1986 mandated that most plans continue to recognize wage and service accruals after the normal retirement age. This legislation reduced the ability of defined-benefit plans to penalize workers who delay retirement.

While details vary, a common attribute of defined-benefit plans is that workers are promised an annuity independent of the level of funding or pension fund investment performance. The most common formula for determining benefits recognizes years of service and earnings. A typical "salary-based" plan would pay a worker reaching the plan's normal retirement age an annuity of 1.5 percent of his highest five-year average earnings for each year of service.[8] "Pattern" plans, almost always found in union settings, deliver a fixed dollar amount per year of service.

Two important defined-benefit plan characteristics concern the distributions of vested benefits to employees who separate before retirement and the adjustment of benefits after retirement. Pension assets in defined-benefit plans generally are "locked in," meaning that vested workers who leave the firm do not receive an immediate lump-sum payment, but must wait until they meet age and service requirements before they begin receiving an annuity.[9] Only 10 percent of workers in defined-benefit plans are eligible to receive all benefits as a lump sum. Defined-contribution assets, in contrast, are available to 80 percent of pre-retirement workers, should they leave the firm (Atkins 1986).

Only a small number of plans formally index annuities to inflation after retirement (Allen, Clark, and McDermed 1992). Informal, ad hoc inflation adjustments were common during the 1970s, but most pension recipients bear substantial inflation risk. Allen, Clark, and Sumner (1986) estimated that while most retirees with defined-benefit annuities received an inflation adjustment between 1973 and 1979, the average adjustment offset only 40 percent of price level increases.

In defined-contribution plans, benefits are determined by the value of the employee's retirement account. Employers make contributions on the employee's behalf, based either upon wages, profits, or both. The lump-sum or annuity depends upon the market value of contributions plus interest and dividend earnings. Thus employees bear more investment risk under defined-contribution plans (however, see Chapter 1, note 5). Defined-contribution plans are, by definition, fully funded, and the costs to the employer are well defined. Defined-contribution benefits are more portable, because of short vesting periods and the widespread availability of lump-sum distributions for workers who leave before reaching retirement age.

Retirement plans historically were synonymous with defined-benefit plans. Defined-contribution plans became prominent as secondary coverage, frequently as part of an incentive or profit-sharing plan. But defined-benefit pensions have experienced a steady and significant loss in market share to defined-contribution plans as the primary coverage; the percentage of covered workers whose primary plan was defined-benefit fell from 87 percent in 1975 to 56 percent by 1993 (see Table 2.2). Most of this decline represents a shift towards defined-contribution plans by plans with fewer than 10 participants. Defined-benefit plans remain popular with large employers, and few sponsors of large defined-benefit plans have replaced them with defined-contribution pensions.[10]

The fastest-growing form of pension coverage is the 401(k) plan. Congress passed tax rules for Cash or Deferred Arrangements (CODAs) in 1978, which allowed employees to make voluntary, pre-tax contributions to an employer-sponsored profit-sharing or salary reduction plan. In the latter, firms can match employee contributions, and 86 percent of 401(k) plans include some matching provision (Papke 1995). Matching allows the firm to reward higher-wage workers, since the latter are more likely to contribute (subject to Internal Revenue Service [IRS] nondiscrimination rules which require that a tax-qualified pension plan not disproportionately favor high-wage employees). Another attractive feature of 401(k) plans is that participants may be allowed to access the funds before retirement, as withdrawals or borrowings.

Growth in 401(k) coverage has been dramatic since the IRS issued regulations in 1982. Between 1984 and 1993, the number of 401(k) plans increased from 17,300 to 154,500, while over the same period the number of participants reached 23.1 million. 401(k) coverage appears to be primarily supplemental, designed to add to a primary defined-benefit or other defined-contribution plan. Only a decade after their initiation, however, 401(k) plans provided primary coverage for 12 percent of the workers who have a pension.[11]

PENSION POLICY IN THE UNITED STATES

Federal policy has been a major influence on private pensions since the first plans were established early in the century. The Internal Revenue Service's basic policy of excluding employer contributions and pension fund earnings from current taxable income was adopted shortly after the corporate and personal income tax. Payments to fund current retirement benefits were recognized as legitimate business deductions for corporations. The Revenue Acts of 1921 and 1926 explicitly exempted the earnings of assets in retirement funds from taxation, and the Revenue Act of 1928 allowed pension sponsors to deduct contributions to advance fund benefit accruals. There is evidence that favorable tax policy encouraged the growth of pensions, especially during the expansion of coverage after World War II (Long and Scott 1982).

More recently, the trend in federal tax policy has been to tighten benefit and contribution ceilings, reducing the preferences accorded pension compensation. Contribution limits were established by the Revenue Act of 1942, in response to fears that pensions were increasingly being adopted for the primary purpose of avoiding income taxation. This legislation also established nondiscrimination rules, which prohibit adoption of pensions for the primary benefit of high-wage employees.

Congress has lowered limits on allowable contributions and benefits several times since 1982. The Tax Equity and Fiscal Responsibility Act of 1982 (TEFRA) reduced the annual benefit that a defined-benefit participant could receive. Benefits paid to defined-benefit participants now are limited to the lesser of 100 percent of the highest three-year average earnings or $125,000. TEFRA also reduced the maximum contribution to defined-contribution plans. These limits were lowered further by the Deficit Reduction Act of 1984 and again in the Tax Reform Act of 1986. Allowable contributions to defined-contribution plans may not exceed 25 percent of an employee's compensation or $30,000.

An overall limit on annual compensation that can be used for benefit determinations became effective in 1989. This compensation limit was lowered from $235,840 to $150,000 in the 1993 Omnibus Budget Reconciliation Act.

Employer contributions to fund benefits also are limited. The Internal Revenue Code allows a deduction for the "normal cost" of accrued benefits plus amortization of any prior unfunded liabilities. Since 1987, contributions to plans having assets equal to or above 150 percent of current liabilities are not deductible and are, instead, subject to a 10 percent excise tax. The Code further limits the range of actuarial assumptions that may be used to calculate pension liabilities. Thus sponsors cannot avoid the 150 percent funding limit by adopting a low discount rate. Contributions to pension funds determined to be overfunded are disallowed. The full funding limit is a controversial rule, as critics argue that it prevents many plans from adequately funding ongoing (rather than termination) liabilities and eliminates the tax shield for many plans (Ippolito 1991b).

The primary motivations for increased taxation of pensions appear to be reducing federal budget deficits and the preference of Congress for broadening the tax base versus raising marginal income tax rates. Some critics have warned that the cumulative effect of reducing pension tax preferences will be greater complexity and reduced attractiveness of pensions, especially defined-benefit plans (Goodfellow and Schieber 1993).

PENSION REGULATION

Before 1975, pension regulation was vested in the federal income tax code, which established conditions for tax-qualified pension plans. The most significant pension regulations were created by The Employee Retirement Income Security Act of 1974 (ERISA). The expressed goal of ERISA was to ensure that promised pension benefits were actually received by retired workers. ERISA created rules for vesting, funding, and investing in defined-benefit plans. One of the more controversial provisions of ERISA was authorization of the Pension Benefit Guaranty Corporation (PBGC) to administer a mandatory federal insurance program for defined-benefit obligations. The PBGC is charged with protecting workers' benefits in the event of bankruptcy of the sponsor of an underfunded pension plan. Critics of the PBGC have argued that premiums are too low and insufficiently experience-rated, resulting in incentives for sponsors to terminate underfunded plans. They also point out that the PBGC subsidizes a small number of plans which are substantially underfunded.

ERISA established vesting rules. The most popular was 10-year cliff vesting, subsequently reduced to five years by the Tax Reform Act of 1986. Vesting rules address only part of the portability issue. We explain in Chapter 3 that even fully vested workers lose substantial pension wealth when changing jobs, even if they immediately begin earning credits in a new defined-benefit plan. Since 1986 several legislative proposals have addressed this problem but none have been enacted (Turner 1993).

Pension portability also is a function of policies that affect the choice between defined-benefit and defined-contribution plans. Some pension analysts have suggested that policies favorable to defined-contribution growth were intended by Congress to promote pension portability (Salisbury 1992). These policies include frequent changes in pension rules concerning reporting, vesting, and nondiscrimination, which have made administering defined-benefit plans more complex, especially for small employers. There is evidence that the price of administering defined-benefit plans relative to defined-contribution pensions has risen, especially for small firms (Hay/Huggins 1990). At the same time, tax preferences for defined-benefit plans have been reduced.[12] Another policy change that has been unfavorable to defined-benefit coverage is the liberalization of tax rules for CODAs. As we have noted, 401(k) plans have been well received.

Falling defined-benefit coverage has attracted considerable attention and concern. Some policymakers fear that growing defined-contribution coverage will lower retirement income. Savings rates in typical defined-contribution plans may be lower than in defined-benefit plans. Also, participants frequently are required to direct their own investments, and evidence suggests that workers choose low-risk, but low-return, portfolios. The most significant concern is that workers generally receive a lump-sum distribution when leaving a defined-contribution plan, and despite recent increases in penalties for failure to roll over into an IRA or a new pension, there is significant preretirement consumption of these assets.[13]

In terms of this study, the major issue raised by the trend to defined-contribution coverage for this study is its implications for the use of defined-benefit pensions as a tool to increase workforce productivity. Does the growing choice of defined-contribution plans imply that productivity effects are of second-order importance? We address this question in Chapter 5.

NOTES

1. Readers interested in more detail can consult Ippolito (1986), Clark and McDermed (1990), or Turner and Beller (1992).
2. As pointed out by Williamson, the view of older workers as more accident-prone turned out to be erroneous.
3. Hannah (1986) reaches a similar conclusion for early pension growth in Great Britain.

4. Apparently, DuPont management also believed that workers would accept lower wages in exchange for the promise of future benefits, thus reducing the cost of the program.

5. See Doescher (1994) or Parsons (1994).

6. Multiemployer plans may continue to use 10-year vesting for employees covered by collective bargaining agreements.

7. "Unreduced" means that the retiree will be eligible for benefits as defined by the benefit formula given that individual's years of service and final average earnings. Of course, the benefit would rise by delaying retirement until age 65 through increased years of service, and perhaps, rising nominal earnings.

8. The "generosity parameter" commonly ranges between 1.25 and 1.75 percent for each year of service (U.S. Department of Labor 1996).

9. An exception is employees who have a small vested benefit. Defined-benefit sponsors may unilaterally cash out employees having vested benefits of less than $3,500.

10. See Silverman and Yakoboski (1994). It should also be noted that the trend away from defined-benefit plans has been much less apparent in Canada. Defined-benefit plans were the primary coverage vehicle for 90 percent of covered workers in 1992 (Statistics Canada 1994).

11. See Papke, Petersen, and Poterba (1993) for detailed analysis of 401(k) coverage and trends.

12. Clark and McDermed (1990) ascribe most of the shift towards defined-contribution plans to changes in pension policy. Gustman and Steinmeier (1992), on the other hand, argue that the dominant factor has been structural changes—the relative decline in traditionally strong defined-benefit sectors of large, unionized, and manufacturing employment.

13. Samwick and Skinner (1994), however, estimate that the typical defined-contribution plan will yield comparable median income compared with defined-benefit plans. They estimate that portability losses from the latter are of similar magnitude to asset reductions resulting from spending lump-sum distributions.

3 Pension Incentives

This chapter describes the nature and source of pension incentives. It is well known that defined-benefit pensions establish penalties for early separation and late retirement. This observation is itself an argument for the productivity theory of pensions, because workers' ability to respond to favorable job opportunities and to continue working past the normal retirement age are valuable career options which workers would not freely forego. Pension separation penalties also add to the risk associated with an involuntary layoff. It follows that these penalties would be accepted by workers in a voluntary employment contract only if they supported productivity gains at least sufficient to allow the firm to fund a wage premium that compensated for constraints on workers' career choices.

A knowledge of pension institutions and the resulting structure of incentives is needed to evaluate whether the productivity theory makes economic sense. The information in this chapter also should allow the reader to understand how legislation would enhance pension benefit portability. Most of the discussion relates to defined-benefit plans. Arguments that defined-contribution plans, including the rapidly growing 401(k)-type pensions, also may provide productive incentives are presented in Chapter 4.

THE PENSION QUIT PENALTY

Pension tenure incentives frequently are attributed to delayed vesting.[1] Before ERISA, defined-benefit plans often made no provision for vesting before retirement. An important part of the legislative history of ERISA are infamous cases in which long-tenured workers were dismissed just prior to retirement and lost all pension wealth.[2] Except for the years just preceding retirement, however, incomplete vesting is a minor component of the pension separation penalty. Even workers who are "fully vested" stand to lose substantial pension wealth if they leave a job before retirement. The pension loss arises primarily because most defined-benefit plans 1) calculate benefits relative to the worker's peak average earnings, and 2) do not index the earnings of workers who leave the plan before they are eligible to receive benefits. A specific example will clarify the source of the pension loss.

David and Norman are two identical 45-year-old employees who have worked continuously for the past 10 years at Zeke's Zippers, Inc. They are fully vested in Zeke's defined-benefit plan. Each draws an annual salary of $40,000 and anticipates retiring at the plan's normal retirement age of 65. Zeke's plan pays an annuity equal to 1.5 percent of the highest three-year average pay times each worker's total years of service. David and Norman each forecast that the nominal interest rate and wage growth will continue at the current rate of 6 percent.

Suppose that Norman, for reasons outside his control, resigns from his job and moves across the country. Norman is vested, so Zeke's is obligated to pay him the full annuity, based on his earnings and service, when Norman reaches age 65.

The annual pension payment is Norman's highest three-year average salary ($37,779, based upon 6 percent nominal wage growth the previous two years) times 1.5 percent times 10 years of service:

$$\$37,779 \times 0.015 \times 10 = \$5,667.$$

The annual annuity of $5,667 can be converted to a lump-sum value of $62,335 by multiplying by a present-value annuity factor of 11.[3]

Fortunately, Norman immediately finds a new job with Fritz' Brickless Fireplaces at his previous wage and with identical pension coverage. Assuming continuous employment with Fritz' through retirement (20 more years) and maintaining the salary growth assumption of 6 percent, Norman will be entitled to an additional pension valued at

$$(\$125,221 \times 0.015 \times 20) \times 11 = \$413,229.$$

The sum of his pension wealth from both employers at age 65 will be $475,564.

David, in contrast, works continuously at Zeke's through age 65. He receives

$$(\$125,221 \times 0.015 \times 30) \times 11 = \$619,844.$$

The pension quit penalty is the difference between David's and Norman's pension wealth. At a nominal interest rate of 6 percent, the present value of the penalty is

$$(\$619{,}844 - \$475{,}564)e^{-0.06(20)} = \$43{,}456.$$

The defined-benefit plan thus establishes a quit penalty equal to 1.09 times each worker's current annual salary, at their current age and service level.[4]

This example clarifies that the source of the pension loss from a quit is not incomplete vesting, a lapse in coverage, or lower earnings at the new job—though these would add to Norman's loss. The penalty arises because his first 10 years of service is weighted by his final average earnings with Zeke's ($37,779), whereas David's entire 30 years of service is weighted by the considerably larger average preretirement earnings ($125,221). Norman's pension from Zeke's is fully vested, but the benefit formula does not index the earnings base. Note that had Norman not been vested in Zeke's pension, he would have received only the pension from Fritz, and his loss would have been larger by $(\$62{,}335)e^{-0.06(20)} = \$18{,}775$, less than half the loss that arises from inflation of the earnings base.

Once a worker achieves full vesting, the pension penalty requires an expectation of nominal wage growth. If nominal wages were fixed, Norman's pension loss would be zero. Neither would there be a penalty if service credits were portable, i.e., if Fritz' plan was required to transfer Norman's 10 years of service credit to its own plan. In fact, defined-benefit plans almost never index the wage base or accept service credit from previous jobs. Thus, the thrust of policy proposals to enhance pension benefit portability is to require indexing or to establish clearinghouses for service credit (Turner 1993).

An important property of the pension quit penalty is its concavity relative to years of service. The curve is concave-down because an early quit allows most years of service to be weighted to the higher earnings on the subsequent job, while for a late quit there is little nominal wage growth before retirement. After five years of service with Zeke, Norman's three-year highest annual salary would have been $27,941, assuming continuous wage growth of 6 percent. Had Norman taken the new job then, his total pension would have had a value at retirement of

$$[(\$27,941 \times 0.015 \times 5) \times 11] + [(\$125,221 \times 0.015 \times 25) \times 11]$$
$$= \$539,588.$$

The present value of the pension loss would have been

$$(\$619,844 - \$539,588)e^{-0.06(25)} = \$17,908,$$

or about 60 percent of current earnings.[5] Under the same assumptions, a quit three years from retirement at age 62, after 27 years with Zeke, would yield a pension loss of 69 percent of the current wage. At the extremes, the quit penalty is zero, both before the first year of service is completed and at the retirement age.

The potential pension loss has been called "backloading," because vested benefits accrue disproportionately in the years just prior to retirement. It also has been likened to an option, because the worker who leaves a pension plan early forfeits the opportunity to add to the value of his or her pension (Lazear and Moore 1988).

More generally, the pension loss (PL) is the difference between the present value of the pension based upon current earnings and the projected earnings at retirement:

$$PL = (W_R g s - W_s g s)e^{-i(R-s)},$$

where W_s and W_R are current and retirement average earnings, respectively; s and R are current and retirement years of service, respectively; g is the pension benefit generosity parameter (0.015 in our example); i is the nominal interest rate; and $R - s$ equals the number of years until retirement.

Assuming that current wages grow at a constant annual rate q, earnings at retirement equals $W_s e^{q(R-s)}$. Ippolito (1985) shows that making this substitution for W_R, the ratio of pension loss to current earnings can be written as

$$PL/W_s = gs(e^{q(R-s)} - 1)e^{-i(R-s)}.$$

This equation identifies nominal wage growth as the source of the pension loss. If $q = 0$, then $PL/W_s = 0$, because a quitting worker's current earnings will equal projected earnings at retirement. Also, the pension loss is zero when $s = 0$ or when $s = R$.

Table 3.1 and Figure 3.1 report calculations of the pension loss per dollar of current earnings relative to years of service, nominal wage growth, and the interest rate (assuming immediate vesting). A concave-down career pension loss profile is apparent. When nominal wage growth and the interest rate each are 6 percent, the loss peaks after 18 years of service at $1.52 per dollar of annual current cash wages. A higher discount rate lowers the present value of all pension benefits for the same level of nominal wage growth, and the pension loss is lower at each year of service. At an interest rate of 10 percent, the loss peaks at $0.88 per dollar of annual earnings.[6]

Table 3.1 also shows that the separation penalty is greater when higher inflation raises both the nominal rate of interest and wage growth. When each of the latter is 10 percent, the pension loss reaches a maximum of $1.81 per dollar of current annual earnings at 18 years of service. The higher loss reflects the underlying reason for the pension loss: the interaction of nominal wage growth and an unindexed wage base.

The basic pattern of the quit penalty is not dependent upon the worker joining a firm at any specific age, although not surprisingly, the pension loss is smaller for the worker who begins accumulating service credits at age 45 (Table 3.2, Figure 3.2). The employee who begins a job at age 25, on the other hand (Table 3.3, Figure 3.3), faces a larger pension loss at any given age than workers with less tenure. Regardless of the starting age, the pension loss is concave-down in service and a positive function of nominal wage growth.

Two other simplifying assumptions are constant nominal wage growth and retirement at age 65. The combined effect of these assumptions produces a significant pension loss for workers who quit or are terminated in their early sixties. If, as evidence suggests, wage growth typically slows, older workers' pension loss will be lower.[7] Almost all defined-benefit plans allow workers to begin receiving benefits at least by age 62. When workers are immediately eligible to draw actuarially equivalent benefits, there is no pension loss. Thus the esti-

Table 3.1 Pension Quit Penalty[a]
(per Dollar of Annual Cash Earnings, Starting Age=35)

Age	Years of service	$i=6\%$ $q=6\%$	$i=10\%$ $q=6\%$	$i=10\%$ $q=10\%$
35	0	$ 0	$ 0	$ 0
38	3	0.397	0.117	0.403
41	6	0.755	0.253	0.787
44	9	1.064	0.401	1.139
47	12	1.308	0.556	1.445
50	15	1.469	0.705	1.681
53	18	1.524	0.824	1.814
56	21	1.446	0.881	1.797
59	24	1.197	0.823	1.564
62	27	0.734	0.569	1.009
65	30	0	0	0

[a]The figures in this table assume a pension generosity parameter of 1.5 percent per year of service, retirement at age 65, 15 years in retirement, and cost-of-living adjustments during retirement to offset half the rate of inflation. Thus when the nominal interest rate is 6 percent (inflation premium of 4 percent), the discount rate for converting the retirement annuity into a lump-sum equivalent is 4 percent. When the nominal interest rate is 10 percent, the discount rate is 6 percent.

Figure 3.1 Pension Quit Penalty, Age 35 Start

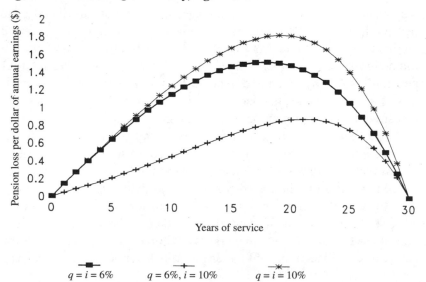

Table 3.2 Pension Quit Penalty[a]
(per Dollar of Annual Cash Earnings, Starting Age=45)

Age	Years of Service	$i=6\%$ $q=6\%$	$i=10\%$ $q=6\%$	$i=10\%$ $q=10\%$
45	0	$ 0	$ 0	$ 0
48	3	0.317	0.139	0.354
51	6	0.563	0.279	0.652
54	9	0.717	0.404	0.866
57	12	0.755	0.479	0.953
60	15	0.641	0.525	0.851
63	18	0.336	0.271	0.470
65	20	0	0	0

[a]See footnote to Table 3.1.

Figure 3.2 Pension Quit Penalty, Age 45 Start

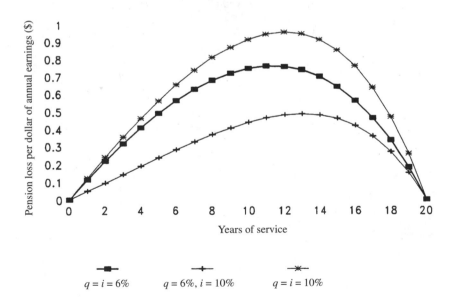

Table 3.3 Pension Quit Penalty[a]
(per Dollar of Annual Cash Earnings, Starting Age=25)

Age	Years of Service	$i=6\%$ $q=6\%$	$i=10\%$ $q=6\%$	$i=10\%$ $q=10\%$
25	0	$ 0	$ 0	$ 0
28	3	0.441	0.087	0.422
31	6	0.861	0.193	0.836
34	9	1.254	0.317	1.239
37	12	1.611	0.460	1.626
40	15	1.923	0.618	1.985
43	18	2.177	0.789	2.308
46	21	2.357	0.963	2.576
49	24	2.444	1.127	2.762
52	27	2.413	1.253	2.833
55	30	2.333	1.308	2.735
58	33	1.867	1.233	2.396
61	36	1.267	0.944	1.711
64	39	0.375	0.315	0.535
65	40	0	0	0

[a]See footnote to Table 3.1.

Figure 3.3 Pension Quit Penalty, Age 25 Start

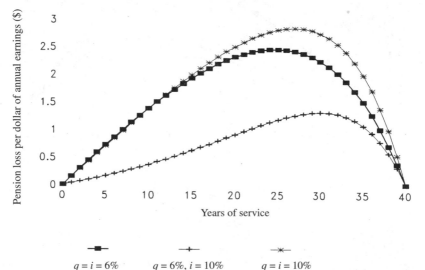

mates in Tables 3.1–3.3 probably overstate the potential losses of pre-retirement age employees.

RETIREMENT INCENTIVES

In a world in which productivity was easily observed and wages were perfectly flexible, firms would not need a retirement policy. When and if an employee's productivity declined below the opportunity cost of his or her time, the falling wage would create the appropriate incentive for voluntary retirement. But if the internal labor market includes an understanding that the wages of senior employees will not be cut, explicit retirement incentives are needed. Resistance to wage cuts may result from implied agreements to discourage shirking (Becker and Stigler 1974), or to shift the risk of falling productivity to the employer. Legislation prohibiting age discrimination also may discourage wage cuts for older workers; however, firms seemed reluctant to cut senior employees' wages well before the Age Discrimination in Employment Act (ADEA) was enacted in 1967.

Many companies employed mandatory retirement rules in preference to cutting the wages of older workers. With the abolition of mandatory retirement by the 1978 amendments to ADEA, voluntary retirement incentives became more important (Mutschler 1996). Establishing a retirement policy is frequently identified by human resource managers as the primary supply-side function for pensions.

The fundamental reason why defined-benefit pensions encourage early retirement is that they provide annuities based upon service and earnings, independent of the value of the pension fund. When the worker is eligible to receive benefits, the accrual in pension value resulting from an additional year of work declines because the annuity is drawn one less year. In fact, additional years of service beyond age 65 generally will lower the present value of benefits. The latter effect was more pronounced prior to 1986, when most pension plans froze service credit and earnings at age 65. At that time, postponing retirement beyond 65 would not increase annual benefits; it only would reduce the time that benefits were received. Plans now must credit additional years of service and recognize wage increases after age 65.

The present value of expected benefits still declines for most workers after normal retirement, however, because few plans provide an actuarial adjustment of benefits upward to reflect fewer years of receipt.

Defined-contribution plans, in contrast, deliver benefits equal to the value of pension fund earnings and contributions. By their nature, the present value of defined-contribution benefits is independent of the age of retirement once the age of eligibility is reached.

There is no inherent reason why defined-benefit plans must reward early retirement. Pension wealth could be made neutral with respect to the retirement age by adjusting benefits upward for workers who delay retirement, just as most plans make a downward actuarial adjustment for early retirement. The U.S. Department of Labor's Employee Benefits Survey (1996) indicates that less than 10 percent of defined-benefit plans grant increased benefits to workers who postpone retirement.

Defined-benefit plans also may encourage workers to leave before the plan's normal retirement age. The Employee Benefits Survey reports that virtually all defined-benefit pensions have provisions for early retirement. While benefits are reduced for workers electing early retirement, the value of the defined-benefit pension commonly is maximized by drawing benefits as soon as eligible. Kotlikoff and Wise (1987) and Lazear (1983) reviewed a large sample of plans and concluded that the expected present value of pensions benefits generally peaked at the earliest age of benefit eligibility.

Other studies have indicated, instead, that the pension value is constant between early and normal retirement ages, especially for plans which base benefits on highest average earnings (Fields and Mitchell 1984). The wage growth assumption is crucial. If older workers anticipate flat or declining *nominal* earnings between the ages of 62 and 65, the value of the pension generally will be maximized by early retirement. Either way, the annual pension accrual drops once the age of early retirement is reached, establishing, in effect, a total compensation cut for continued work.

Defined-benefit pensions also are well-suited to special early retirement buyouts. The Employee Benefits Survey reported that 25 to 40 percent of defined-benefit plans contained provisions allowing workers who do not meet regular age and service requirements to begin drawing vested pension benefits immediately in the event of a plant closing. A survey by Doescher and Dorsey (1992) found that older workers in a plant closing or "downsizing" generally received an ad hoc pension bonus in the form of additional years of service credit or the right to begin drawing vested benefits immediately. Luzadis and Mitchell (1991) reported an increasing trend toward early retirement incentives in defined-benefit plans and found evidence consistent with the theory that defined-benefit pensions are used to establish "buyouts" for older employees. Defined-benefit pensions, in effect, provide severance pay for older displaced workers.

Could employers establish retirement incentives with defined-contribution plans or even nonpension cash bonuses? Of course, but there appear to be two reasons why employers prefer defined-benefit retirement incentives. First, such incentives are automatic and inherent attributes of the way retirement benefits are delivered under defined-benefit plans. Plan sponsors must incorporate an actuarial upward benefit adjustment in order to prevent defined-benefit plans from penalizing older workers. Defined-contribution plans, in contrast, are retirement-age neutral. Firms with these pensions would have to levy explicit penalties on older workers, which would risk being seen as discriminatory. Rather than fine older workers who fail to retire, employers could establish a declining schedule of retirement bonuses, but discriminatory interpretations of such an explicit schedule clearly are possible.

Second, and perhaps more importantly, the after-tax cost of establishing retirement incentives is lower under a defined-benefit plan. Contributions to fund early retirement obligations are considered part of the normal cost of the defined-benefit plan and are deductible under Internal Revenue Service rules. Cash bonuses, on the other hand, would be in effect deferred wages and contributions to fund these would not be deductible. In order to meet these obligations, the firm would have to save outside of the pension fund, earning a lower net rate of return.

SUMMARY

Defined-benefit pension incentives for continuous tenure and early retirement create a window of time during which a job separation maximizes the value of pension benefits. An earlier separation lowers pension wealth because the earnings base is not indexed and service credits are not generally portable. These portability losses occur even for fully vested workers. There is a penalty for leaving the firm too late as well, because defined-benefit pension wealth is a function of the size of an annuity and the length of time it is received rather than of the capital value of a pension fund. Employers provide early retirement incentives by not making the appropriate actuarial adjustments that would make the pension value independent the age of retirement. Most plans reduce benefits for early retirement, but they almost never apply an upward adjustment for late retirement. Early retirement incentives outside of defined-benefit plans are awkward, tax-disadvantaged, and may be seen as discriminatory.

Incentives for long tenure or early retirement could be avoided should more neutral plans be preferred. Defined-contribution plans which access tax benefits are, of course, an option favored by most sponsors, but defined-benefit plans could include rules that temper or eliminate tenure and retirement incentives. Given these alternatives, it is worth considering that defined-benefit career incentives might be grounded in productivity gains. In the following chapter, we consider whether pension incentives make sense within the most common internal labor market models.

NOTES

1. For example, Blinder (1982) developed a model of specific training in which the firm uses a pension to discourage quits until it fully recoups its investment, when workers become fully vested. Carmichael (1989) recognized pensions as a tool to establish self-enforcing implicit employment contracts but suggested that early vesting regulations reduced its effectiveness for this purpose.
2. See the summary of Senate testimony on ERISA in (U.S. Senate 1976).
3. This factor assumes 15 years of retirement and a discount rate of 4 percent. The latter is based upon a real interest rate of 2 percent, an inflation premium of 4 percent, and the assumption that the retirement annuity will be adjusted to offset half of the assumed inflation rate, as suggested by Allen, Clark, and Sumner (1986).
4. The quit penalty is smaller if we assume no postretirement indexing of benefits, because the value of all pensions will be lower. Without indexing, the appropriate discount rate for valuing the pension annuity will be the nominal rate of 6 percent, resulting in an annuity factor of 9.7, and the pension loss will be 12 percent smaller than under our original assumption of 50 percent postretirement inflation indexing.

5. If he were not vested after five years, his loss would have been higher by $5,143. Again, lack of vesting plays a small part in establishing the quit penalty.

6. A higher discount rate lowers pension wealth and losses for two reasons. The present value of the lump-sum equivalent is less, but also since we have assumed imperfect inflation indexing of retirement annuities, higher nominal interest rates reduce the value of the annuity at retirement.

7. Of course, the assumption that the worker immediately finds another job with equivalent wages and pension benefits is less realistic for older workers, especially for those who experience an involuntary layoff. However, these losses should be attributed to whatever factors are responsible for reduced employment opportunities for older workers, not the pension plan on a previous job. Most older displaced workers, in addition, received special pension rights which offset or eliminate pension losses from an involuntary separation (Doescher and Dorsey 1992).

4 Pension Incentives and Internal Labor Markets

Much of the empirical literature on private pensions has centered on testing whether workers respond to tenure and retirement incentives. The evidence generally suggests that they do. Workers who are covered by a pension are less likely to quit, and retirement decisions are sensitive to differences in pension values.[1] While it seems that workers rationally respond to pension incentives, there is considerably less evidence on the question of why firms put such inducements into place.

The remainder of this monograph addresses the economic function of pension incentives. The productivity perspective is motivated by the recognition that constraints on quit and retirement choices are costly to workers and thus must be justified by other benefits. Internal labor market models assume that workers are more productive in long-term employment relationships. Incentives are needed to preserve job-specific rents and to signal the appropriate time to retire when the match is no longer productive. Pensions can be a vehicle both for penalizing quits and for delivering severance payments at the appropriate retirement age.

In this chapter, we ask whether the incentives described in the preceding chapter are consistent with models in which durable firm-employee relationships generate productivity gains. Labor economists are familiar with the idea that pension incentives may provide benefits in the form of reduced turnover and early retirement,[2] but there has not been a detailed comparison of pension incentives and the incentives implied by internal labor market models. This chapter reviews these models and considers whether pension incentives are consistent. An important question is, Why do firms sponsor pensions over other incentive schemes such as deferred wages? We also consider a self-selection model in which defined-contribution pensions can attract more productive employees.

Our analysis suggests a plausible case for pension incentives in jobs where firm-specific investments or reduced shirking raise productivity. Defined-benefit pensions, however, are not the ideal incentive. The separation penalty may be too weak to preserve a productive match, while at other times it may discourage a worker from leaving for a better match.

THE ECONOMICS OF INTERNAL LABOR MARKETS AND PENSIONS

Twenty-five years ago, the analysis of labor markets was based primarily on an auction-market perspective, under which wage and employment issues were studied within a contemporaneous demand and supply framework. Since then, most important insights into employment, unemployment, and wage determination have been generated from an implicit-contract framework. In the latter, there is a presumption of productive long-term relationships between workers and firms. When long-term employment yields shared gains, an internal labor market is said to exist. Recent economic analysis of internal labor markets has suggested that many workplace institutions can be explained as attempts to achieve efficient outcomes when wages and employment are insulated from contemporaneous demand and supply shifts or when information about productivity is imperfect.

The internal labor market model naturally raises questions about the economic functions of pensions, because establishing appropriate incentives is a key problem. Here we consider whether pension incentives are consistent with three variants of the internal labor market: the firm-specific training theory, the principal-agent or "shirking" model, and an asymmetric information hiring model. Incentives for long tenure are important in each, and retirement bonuses are predicted by the first two. The asymmetric information model suggests that defined-contribution plans also may provide important useful incentives.

Firm-Specific Training Model

The theory of firm-specific training is one of the most widely applied ideas in labor economics. Many jobs involve significant hiring costs and require training in production methods that are not transferable to another firm. These fixed costs generate rents that both parties benefit from preserving. Firm-specific training supports most implicit contract models; Hall (1980) has called it the "glue" that holds workers and firms together.

An implication of firm-specific rents is the need for incentives to discourage workers from quitting and employers from initiating lay-offs. Becker (1964) and, more formally, Hall and Lazear (1984) suggested that an efficient compensation policy divides the rent by setting the wage between the worker's value of marginal product (VMP) and opportunity wage, W^o. When $VMP > W > W^o$, each party benefits from preserving the job match.

Such a rent-sharing scheme creates other problems, however. The quasi-rent creates a bilateral monopoly such that each party has an incentive to try to "hold up" the other (Kennan 1979). The worker could renegotiate the wage up to VMP, if he or she credibly threatens to quit. Similarly, the employer may try to force the wage down to the opportunity wage by threatening a layoff. Most significantly, the threat of a hold-up will generally preclude wage renegotiation in response to shifts in productivity inside and outside the firm when information is asymmetric (Flanagan 1984).

Suppose the alternative wage rises above W, but the employee still is more productive in the current job ($VMP > W^o > W$). Both parties benefit by preserving the job match, but if the employer cannot verify the outside offer it will not raise the wage, fearing an opportunistic claim by the employee. Similarly, the employee will not be receptive to a lower wage in the event productivity at the firm declines. Imperfect information and costly contract renegotiation argue for a fixed wage to divide the job rent.

A cost of a fixed-wage implicit contract is excessive quits and lay-offs unless severance taxes or payments can be established. In the language of implicit contracts, severance payments are needed to make the contract "self-enforcing."

The problems encountered in establishing self-enforcing fixed-wage implicit contracts are well documented.[3] Employers must be able to make a credible commitment to deliver severance payments to employees, with the result that they would only benefit from discharging a worker whose productivity fell below his or her alternative wage. Symmetrically, workers must accept a quit penalty equal to the employer's share of the job rent. A penalty equal to $VMP - W$ eliminates the employee's incentive to attempt a hold-up or to quit unless the alternative wage rises above VMP. If the worker must pay the employer VMP – W, he or she will quit only if the gain in wages exceeds the penalty, i.e., if the wage in the next job exceeds VMP.

In his ground-breaking analysis, Becker (1964) suggested that unvested pensions may serve the economic function of insuring firms against firm-specific human capital losses when workers quit. Firms are more likely to share the costs and benefits of training if it is feasible to establish a severance tax to discourage opportunistic wage bargaining or quits.[4] That pensions facilitate productivity gains by encouraging workers and firms to invest in firm-specific training has been a frequent assumption in research on the economics of pensions.[5]

The training model also implies retirement incentives. A downward-inflexible wage establishes a need for severance payments when productivity falls. In an auction-market model, where the wage equals marginal product continuously, retirement inducements are unnecessary. Falling wages provide the appropriate exit signal for retirement when productivity declines below the alternative value of workers' time. But if the wage is fixed, either to minimize bargaining costs or to provide incentives for effort, workers will have an incentive to stay too long.

Prior to the legislative abolition of mandatory retirement, many employment contracts required workers to resign upon reaching a certain age. In the absence of these rules, severance payments are needed to induce workers to retire voluntarily.[6] Workers will choose to retire if offered a payment that compensates for the loss of future rents—the difference between their wage and alternative value of time. It will be in the interest of firms to offer severance payments when, and if, the worker's productivity drops below his or her value of time.

Lazear (1983) formally has modeled defined-benefit retirement incentives as severance payments. The economic basis for the contract in his analysis is gains from reduced shirking, but severance payments are necessary when older workers' wages are rigid downward for any reason. Firms may promise not to reduce older workers' wages as part of a risk-sharing contract or because asymmetric information makes it difficult for employees to verify diminished productivity. More simply, legislation prohibiting age discrimination effectively may prohibit wage cuts. In each of these cases, pension retirement incentives promote efficiency and productivity by encouraging individuals with diminished capacity to retire.

The severance pay function of pensions, like the quit penalty, encourages investments in workers. In jobs that require training, the career productivity profile is more concave due to depreciation of skills. Also, wages are more likely to be downward-inflexible in an employment contract where there are firm-specific rents. Thus, early retirement inducements should be more common in jobs that require investments in firm-specific training.

The Principal-Agent (or Shirking) Model

Another influential internal labor market model is based upon gains from increased employee effort. Becker and Stigler (1974) first suggested deferred compensation as a solution to the principal-agent problem of ensuring that employees deliver the expected quality of work. Edward Lazear (1979) extended its implications to an economic theory of mandatory retirement. This model assumes high costs of supervising and monitoring employees. If productivity cannot be easily measured (unlike, say, for salespersons or stonemasons), the incentive for individuals to work hard is diminished. Instead, there is an incentive to "shirk," to everyone's mutual loss.

One solution to the principal-agent problem is close employee supervision. The costs of monitoring employees may outweigh the gains of greater output, however. The Becker-Stigler solution establishes a long-term employment contract with deferred compensation. The firm pays the worker less than the value of his or her output early in the career but promises a compensating wage premium to long-tenured employees. Steepening the career wage profile in effect establishes a bond that is forfeited if the employee is dismissed for shirking. Productivity rises through greater effort, and the gains are shared with long-tenured workers.

Pensions enter this model in two ways: as a preferred vehicle for establishing deferred compensation and to enforce the end of the contract when mandatory retirement rules are forbidden. Significant tax advantages apply when compensation is deferred through a defined-benefit pension. As we have seen, employer contributions to a pension fund are not subject to taxation as current profits, and pension dividends and interest (unlike earnings from a deferred wage fund) are not taxed until employees are paid. Also, Ippolito (1991a) points out that steepening an already upward-sloping wage profile results in a higher lifetime tax burden under a progressive income tax.

Another reason for deferring compensation through a pension is that the employer's promise to deliver deferred compensation must be credible in order to establish an effective incentive. Lazear (1979) argued that the cost of reputation damage would discourage employers from reneging on the promise of higher wages late in the worker's career. We argue that reputation capital will be more effective in preventing such opportunistic behavior in a pension contract than in a promise of future wage increases. To avoid deferred pension obligations, employers must systematically fire workers near retirement. But this type of opportunistic behavior is more explicit and easier to detect than failing to raise real wages at an implicit rate. Empirical evidence indicates that the defined-benefit pension promise is credible: workers with pensions are less likely to be discharged than are older workers who are uncovered (Cornwell, Dorsey, and Mehrzad 1991).[7] Ippolito (1991a) showed that pensions have a greater effect on increasing job tenure than does increasing the steepness of the wage profile.

The deferred compensation solution also requires an incentive to keep employees from working too long. Long-tenured workers receive substantial rents and, if permitted, will continue working after their productivity drops below the value of alternative uses of their time. As in the firm-specific training model, severance payments can buy out older workers in the absence of mandatory retirement.[8]

Asymmetric Information Hiring Model

Ippolito (forthcoming) has argued that pensions could raise worker quality and productivity, independent of training or effort incentives, by attracting a higher-quality workforce. This model is based upon three assumptions. First, there are important differences in workers' internal rate of discount. Some are less focused on immediate gratification and instead place a greater value on future rewards; others are more impatient ("high discounters"). Second, employers prefer to hire workers with low discount rates. Workers who have a longer horizon possess several desirable attributes: they are absent from work less, take better care of capital equipment, and are more willing to invest in training and their own reputation to gain future promotions and wage increases. Low discounters thus should require less monitoring and be more responsive to deferred incentives. The third, and crucial, assumption is that the internal discount rate of prospective hires is not observable by employers. A solution to this information asymmetry has the firm promising deferred compensation at a level sufficient to match the opportunity wage of a low discounter. Workers who heavily discount the future therefore self-select out of the applicant pool, because the high discounter's value of the compensation package is below the opportunity wage. Again, pensions are a tax-preferred vehicle for deferring compensation.

Our discussion of pension incentives so far has focused entirely on defined-benefit plans, reflecting the apparent neutrality of defined-contribution plans: early vesting, full portability, and independence of pension value to the age of retirement. This suggests that defined-contribution plans will be chosen by firms that want to provide a tax-favored retirement savings vehicle but where productivity gains from long tenure are low. But unlike the firm-specific training and shirking models, the asymmetric information model implies output gains from sponsoring a defined-contribution pension. For purposes of screening out high discounters, Ippolito argues that defined-contribution pensions are superior to defined-benefit plans. Either plan defers compensation, but the defined-contribution plan also encourages self-correcting quits by high-discount workers who are hired mistakenly.

The advantage of defined-contribution plans is, ironically, their portability. A high discounter may mistakenly be offered and accept a job with a pension. Such a hiring error would not be surprising, given that a high-discount worker will invest less in a job search. He or she places little value on contributions to a pension fund and would prefer greater current wages. Under a defined-contribution plan, a lump sum payout is available to workers who quit early. This incentive encourages high discounters to leave. As we have seen, immediate lump-sum payouts are much more common in defined-contribution plans. While both plans attract low discounters, the defined-contribution plan is more likely to provide an incentive for high discounters who pass through the initial screen to quit.

The authorization and growth of 401(k) type plans magnifies the selection effects of defined-contribution plans. Employees are allowed to make pre-tax contributions to 401(k) plans, which employers generally match up to a limit. The employer match creates, in effect, a wage premium targeted at workers who contribute to the limit, i.e., low discounters.

ARE PENSION TENURE INCENTIVES CONSISTENT WITH THESE MODELS?

Pension incentives appear, at first glance, to be consistent with widely recognized models of productivity gains from long tenure. Further analysis is required, however, to determine whether pension career incentives are efficient. It is possible that pension quit penalties may be too large—that is, greater than the value of the job match to the employer—and thus result in too few quits. At other times, pension incentives may be too weak to discourage an unproductive quit. One test of the productivity theory of pensions is to compare pension incentives with ideal deferred compensation structures.

The firm-specific training model calls for a separation penalty equal to the value of the firm's investment in the employee. This implies that the quit penalty should be concave-down in tenure. A well-established result is that the optimal profile of the stock of human capital is concave (Ben-Porath 1967). The stock of skills grows initially because a high proportion of earnings capacity is devoted to training. Time in training declines with tenure, however, and beyond some point depreciation causes the stock of skills to decline. Assuming that the division between the firm and employee of the returns to specific investments is not dependent upon age or tenure, the capital value of the firm's investment also is concave-down. The optimal quit penalty thus is roughly consistent with the profile of the typical defined-benefit pension quit penalty, as shown in Figures 3.1–3.3.

Of course, not all on-the-job training is acquired as gradually as the firm-specific training model implies. Survey evidence suggests that formal training for many workers is completed within a few years.

Pensions would be not as well suited to discourage quits of workers who receive training in basic skills that are quickly imparted.

In jobs with high initial training outlays but with little ongoing investment in skills, the firm's investment peaks early in the worker's tenure and the pension quit penalty would be too small to deter all inefficient quits. Pension incentives conform more closely to the optimal separation penalty in jobs where training and productivity growth continue well into the career. Defined-benefit pension incentives are more efficient in jobs where training is in large part a matter of acquiring experience and judgement, i.e., "learning by doing." Such informal and gradual accumulation of skills also is more likely to be firm-specific.

The defined-benefit separation penalty seems less suited to the principal-agent model than to the firm-specific training model. Its principal weakness applies to deferred-compensation incentives in general. Akerlof and Katz (1989) argue that deferred compensation is a poor substitute for monitoring because the value of deferred wages is too small to deter shirking by new hires. We have seen that the pension loss is low for workers with low tenure. Akerlof and Katz do not claim that deferred compensation does not discourage shirking. Their critique does suggest, however, that separation penalties must be combined with an alternative incentive, perhaps an efficiency wage, to establish a sufficient penalty for new hires.

PENSION INCENTIVES, PRODUCTIVITY SHOCKS, AND INFLATION

Even if the defined-benefit pension initially preserves productive job matches, an unexpected drop in productivity could cause the quit penalty to become an impediment to efficient quits. Productivity shocks, within and outside the firm, may render previously valuable employment relationships unproductive. As stated by Sherwin Rosen (1985, p. 1170), "Not all marriages are made in heaven. Firms go bankrupt, demand shifts to other locations, supply shifts to other countries, products become obsolete and relative demands for goods have been known to change over time. Contracts call for permanent dissolutions when quasi-rents on firm-specific human capital fall to zero."

An inflexible incentive results in too few quits when firm-specific rents unexpectedly decline. The ideal penalty declines with productivity within the firm. If productivity falls below the worker's alternative wage, a layoff becomes efficient and the appropriate incentive is a severance payment. The loss from leaving a job with a defined-benefit pension before retirement generally is not conditional, however. One might imagine that it would be difficult to write a separation penalty conditional on product demand, due to better information held by the employer.

A more feasible approach might be to differentiate workers who are laid off from voluntary quits. There can be no productive reason for levying a severance tax on workers who are laid off; to the contrary, a fixed quit penalty would hinder separations initiated by the firm. Pension rules could waive the separation penalty for workers who are laid off by, for example, providing for immediate vesting and indexing of the wage base. The full pension loss thus would be felt only by workers who quit.[9]

A review of pension rules and practices by Doescher and Dorsey (1992) found almost no evidence of formal rules that differentiated between workers who are laid off and voluntary quits or, more ambitiously, that linked the pension loss to shifts in productivity. These findings are consistent with the implicit contract literature, which suggests the difficulty of making the pension loss conditional on the point of who initiates the separation. The problem is similar to achieving optimal severance payments in fixed-wage contracts.[10] A variable separation penalty would not be feasible if the employer has better information about the employee's productivity. As long as the firm receives a rent, it has an incentive to overstate the quitting worker's value, thus maximizing the pension transfer. If the worker cannot verify productivity shifts, the risk of opportunistic behavior renders the variable penalty unfeasible.

Moral hazards also may arise. If the separation penalty were conditional upon a layoff, workers who receive a wage offer above their current wage have an incentive to lower their productivity to induce the employer to initiate the separation. Similarly, when productivity declines enough to justify a layoff, the firm would benefit from establishing such disagreeable work conditions that the employee quits. A contract which created such perverse incentives would be in neither party's interest. Finally, if the separation penalty is intended to discourage shirking, the contract would have to distinguish between layoffs due to changes in market conditions and discharges for "cause." Workers dismissed with prejudice must suffer a loss, but this creates an incentive for the employer to opportunistically claim that the worker was shirking (Lazear 1983).[11]

Under certain circumstances, however, these informational and incentives problems would carry less force. The Doescher and Dorsey study reported that older workers who were part of a large layoff or plant closing generally received favorable benefit adjustments and severance payments. Special early retirement benefits, both ad hoc and contractual (primarily in union settings), were frequently observed, and these reduced or offset pension losses of older workers affected by a mass layoff. The pension separation penalty actually is more flexible than formal plan rules suggest.

Nevertheless, the pension loss is not fully flexible in the face of productivity shifts, especially for workers below age 50. Critics of nonportable pensions are correct that pensions can impede efficient mobility out of firms in declining industries. The "industrial feudalism" perspective, however, ignores the opposite problem: too many quits from jobs which contain firm-specific rents without some type of separation penalty. If productivity unexpectedly rises or the job match is better than expected, the separation penalty is too small. Given information problems which prevent first-best, self-enforcing implicit contracts, the pension separation penalty may be a compromise between preserving the benefits of productive job matches and the cost of too little mobility if job rents unexpectedly decline.[12]

INFLATION AND PENSION LOSSES

A increase in the rate of inflation also can result in pension losses that are too high. The examples in Chapter 3 showed that the pension loss is sensitive to the nominal wage inflation rate. Indeed, anticipation of growth in wages is the source of the separation penalty. But neither the job training nor the principal-agent model calls for greater real separation penalties when inflation escalates. The real value of the firm's investment in workers, as well as the optimal shirking penalty, should be independent of inflation.

Why is the pension quit penalty sensitive to inflation? Ippolito (1986) notes that Internal Revenue Service rules explicitly prohibit the skewing of pension benefits to senior employees. Tying benefits to earnings may be the only way to backload benefits in a tax-qualified plan.

This second-best solution would seem to work best under an expectation of stable inflation rates. Quit penalties that were appropriate for workers who joined firms during the 1950s and early 1960s would have been excessive during the 1970s. Of course, firms could have reacted to higher and more variable inflation by adding rules that would have partially indexed the wage base for employees who separated before they were eligible to receive benefits. This would have prevented an increase in portability losses when inflation rose above some threshold level. The puzzle is why partial indexing features did not appear during the period of more volatile inflation.

SUMMARY

Defined-benefit pensions clearly convey important career incentives. The fundamental issue is whether pension incentives are systematically related to productivity gains from durable employment relationships. This chapter has reviewed the most widely cited long-term employment models and considered whether pensions incentives make sense within these frameworks. We find that pension tenure incentives for long tenure are consistent with the firm-specific training model, when skills accumulate gradually. Defined-benefit pensions also have advantages in creating deferred compensation in the principal-agent model. In any scenario where wages are downward-inflexible for older workers, defined-benefit plans can play a important role in establishing severance payments.

Pension incentives are not the theoretic ideal. The quit penalty may be too weak for new hires, especially if training is completed early in the job. Others have argued that pension penalties are too large and impede efficient job changes when within-firm productivity falls. An unexpected rise in inflation also can create excessive quit penalties. In these situations, inflexible pension penalties discourage efficient labor mobility.

On the other hand, similar problems apply to up-front bonds or deferred wages. The implicit-contract literature suggests that it will be difficult in general to establish efficient severance taxes and payments. Thus, employment arrangements must trade off the gains from long tenure against the costs of preserving unproductive job matches if economic conditions change.

While most of our discussion has been in terms of defined-benefit plans, incentives also can be conveyed by defined-contribution pensions. Any deferred compensation scheme attracts employees with low discount rates. But defined-contribution lump-sum payouts also encourage high-discount workers who are mistakenly hired to quit, and 401(k) plans permit wage premiums to be targeted to low discounters.

NOTES

1. Evidence on quits and pensions includes Allen, Clark, and McDermed (1993), Gustman and Steinmeier (1995), and Even and Macpherson (1996). Empirical studies of pension incentives and retirement are found in Fields and Mitchell (1984) and Stock and Wise (1990).
2. However, economists also are quick to point out that incentives to discourage quits may be an impediment to efficient labor mobility: for example, Ross (1958), Choate and Linger (1986), and Ehrenberg and Smith (1997). The implicit assumption is that no job-specific rent is present and thus any incentive for long tenure could preserve unproductive job matches.
3. See Arnott, Hosios, and Stiglitz (1988) or Ito (1988), for example.
4. Much of the literature on self-enforcing contracts focuses on problems arising from the difficulty of establishing separation penalties on workers. It is noted that up-front cash bonds are not feasible due to imperfect capital markets and are in fact seldom observed. The potential role of pensions generally is ignored, however, beyond reference to Becker's suggestion about the role of unvested pensions. For example, Carmichael (1989) notes that while pensions at one time might have established feasible quit penalties, legislation reducing the vesting period has eliminated this role. However, Chapter 2 makes it clear that even fully vested pensions establish quit penalties.
5. Examples of papers that suggest that pensions are motivated, at least in part, by firm-specific training are Rice (1966), Schiller and Weiss (1979), Blinder (1982),

Long and Scott (1982), Ippolito (1991a), Woodbury and Bettinger (1991), and Allen, Clark, and McDermed (1993).

6. In Japan, mandatory retirement still is widely used to enforce the end of long-term employment contracts. However, many Japanese workers continue to work for their lifetime employer after mandatory retirement, but at sharply lower wages (Turner and Watanabe 1995).

7. Another factor making the pension promise more credible is federal insurance. Since 1975, the pension contract has been partially insured by the Pension Benefit Guaranty Corporation. Mandatory PBGC insurance reduces the likelihood that pension benefits would not be received due to firm bankruptcy. This insurance does not appear to have made defined-benefit pensions more widespread, however. Defined-benefit pensions reached their peak of popularity before the enactment of ERISA.

8. Another role for pensions is to discourage shirking by employees who are very close to retirement. Since their deferred wage losses from dismissal are small, Lazear argues that the threat of lost pension rights could prevent more extreme forms of shirking, such as theft. It is unlikely, however, that employers could credibly threaten to withhold pension benefits to older workers who did not put forth sufficient effort.

9. This would still result in too few quits if productivity falls, but the firm continues to earn a quasi-rent on the employee. Some workers could receive a wage offer greater than their current productivity but not enough to offset a pension loss that reflected a higher value to the job match.

10. See, for example, Holmstrom (1983), Hall and Lazear (1984), Kahn (1985), Ito (1988), and Arnott, Hosius, and Stiglitz (1988).

11. The problem of establishing the appropriate separation penalty that establishes separation efficiency is essentially the same as that of providing for optimal severance payments in implicit contracts. The literature suggests that it will in general be impossible to achieve first-best severance payments (Ito 1988).

12. While nonportable pensions are criticized for tying workers to jobs, it seems likely that quit penalties established by deferred wages or efficiency wages also would have to be inflexible. If pensions were required to be perfectly portable, employers may substitute deferred wage incentives, which also would result in insufficient mobility out of declining industries.

5 Empirical Evidence on Pensions and Productivity

The preceding chapter outlined what we believe is a sound basis for arguing that pension incentives can promote higher labor productivity, but competing perspectives on pensions emphasize insurance, tax avoidance, and other "demand-side" motives. These perspectives and the productivity theory of pensions are not mutually exclusive. One certainly could believe that the primary purpose of pensions is to encourage tax-preferred retirement savings, while recognizing that firms also benefit from incentives. Demand-side models have received more attention, and some writers go so far as to characterize pension tenure incentives as lowering productivity by locking workers into their current jobs. The implication of pensions being costly must be that the incentives are unintended.

We question whether pension incentives can be both costly and unintended. If nonportable retirement benefits discourage workers from accepting jobs with higher current wages, it would be in employers' interests to avoid imposing such costs unless lower mobility was valuable. Chapter 3 described how sponsors could write pension rules to make benefits independent of tenure. The quit penalty could be avoided by indexing the earnings of workers who separate before retirement. Alternatively, employers could provide immediate lump-sum distributions of vested benefits using a real discount rate.

Indexation of the wage base is almost never observed in private pensions, however, and lump-sum distributions from defined-benefit plans are not common (Turner 1993). When lump-sums are provided, they are valued using a nominal interest rate, which does not eliminate the portability loss due to inflation.

Sponsors also could raise portability by early vesting. Recall from Chapter 2 that vesting rates were low before ERISA and subsequent regulations. The lack of voluntary early vesting makes sense only if employers believed that lower turnover is productive.[1] A similar argument can be made for early retirement incentives. Plan sponsors could provide pensions that are actuarially fair for all retirement ages, but this practice seldom is observed. In fact, plan sponsors exhibited a preference for stronger retirement incentives until regulations mandated crediting service after the normal retirement age.

The persistence of pension backloading, delayed vesting, and early retirement bonuses is circumstantial evidence that pensions raise productivity.[2] But does direct empirical evidence supports the productivity theory of pensions? The remainder of this monograph addresses this question. We begin in this chapter by reviewing previous econometric studies. There are few direct tests of pensions' effect on productivity, but several papers provide indirect evidence. This chapter concludes with a discussion of the implications of the well-known growth in primary coverage by defined-contribution plans. This trend raises the question of whether the productivity gains supported by traditional defined-benefit incentives are no longer important.

DIRECT ECONOMETRIC EVIDENCE

Productivity gains frequently are cited by labor economists as a reason for pensions, but there is virtually no direct evidence that pension incentives improve employee or firm performance. Gustman and Mitchell (1992) cite a familiar culprit: inadequate data. Productivity studies long have been hampered by the lack of direct measures of employee output or firm productivity, and the endogenous nature of pension coverage results in even more stringent data requirements. Even longitudinal data may not suffice, because changes in pension coverage may be endogenous (see Chapter 7).

Despite these difficulties, Allen and Clark (1987) made a first attempt at examining the pension/productivity relationship. The authors estimated a productivity equation across three-digit industries. Value added per worker was regressed against the capital/labor ratio, union membership, firm size, average age and schooling, and the percentage of industry workers covered by a pension. They found no relationship between the extent of pension coverage and productivity measures by industry in general. However, more extensive pension coverage was associated with higher productivity in industries having low union membership, younger age composition, and a lower hiring rate. They also found no evidence that differences in pension coverage were significantly correlated with productivity growth, return on equity, or profit margins. The authors were aware that the estimates suffered from the shortcomings discussed above. Their productivity data is highly aggregated and they did not attempt to model the endogeneity of pension coverage across industries. Indeed, such a two-stage procedure would not have been feasible with available data.

In a paper primarily focused on employment fluctuations and profit sharing, Kruse (1991) estimated employment elasticities with respect to wages and pension costs. His results also can be viewed as a test of the productivity effect of pensions, because higher pension costs should reflect more generous pensions and greater incentives. In effect, this variable combines compensation costs with a shift parameter for labor quality. If pension-covered workers are more productive, the pension cost elasticity should be smaller (less negative) than the wage elasticity. In other words, higher pension costs would be offset by greater productivity, leading to a smaller drop in employment.

Kruse estimated labor demand functions for a sample of firms taken from the CompuStat file matched with Form 5500 pension plan reports. Coefficients on the pension variable were generally smaller than wage coefficients, but the hypothesis that the elasticities were equal could not be rejected. Evidence of equal elasticities implies that higher pension costs are not associated with an increase in the productivity of labor.[3]

Compensation Policies and Productivity

The absence of direct econometric evidence on pension incentives and worker productivity is understandable in light of the ambitious data needs. The human resource literature also has generated no evidence on pensions and productivity. In fact, until recently there have been few formal econometric studies of the incentive effects of compensation policies in general, so the lack of direct evidence on pensions and productivity must be understood in the larger context of our ignorance of the productivity effects of wage premiums, wage ladders, merit pay, and bonuses.

Recent research by labor economists and human resource specialists has begun to address this deficiency. Most of the initial studies of compensation and productivity came from the finance literature. A comprehensive review of the literature by Ehrenberg and Milkovich (1987) found a number of studies that reported a positive correlation between executive compensation and changes in firm performance, and there was a consensus that the adoption of stock options and profit-based compensation schemes is associated with positive abnormal stock returns. Their review yielded little evidence on the impact of compensation systems for non-executive employees, however. A few studies examined the relationship between wage levels and measures of performance such as absenteeism and turnover, but none tested for the effects of seniority-based wage structures. Ehrenberg and Milkovich concluded that very little could be said about the incentive effects of merit pay schemes because of methodological flaws in existing studies. They summarized the state of knowledge: "We do not know if a firm's pay position relative to its competitors, the number of pay grades it offers, pay differentials between these grades, or the profile of employees in a firm's pay hierarchy have any effect on employee behavior or the firm's economic performance" (p. 112).

A notable advance in the pay/productivity literature was a special 1990 issue of *Industrial and Labor Relations Review*, "Do Compensation Policies Matter?" edited by Ronald Ehrenberg. This volume included papers that examined the effect of alternative compensation systems for non-executive employees. Lawrence Kahn and Peter Sherer (1990) estimated a positive and significant correlation between the sensitivity of pay to performance and subsequent performance ratings of middle- and upper-level managers. Beth Asch (1990) presented evidence that production employees respond to incentives. She found that the output of navy recruiters, in terms of the quantity and quality of new recruits, varied over the tour of duty to maximize the likelihood of winning a prize. Recruiters nearing the end of their tour, with little chance of earning a prize, sharply reduced their output.

A Brookings Institution project (Blinder 1990) also presented new evidence on productivity and individual incentives. Notably, Mitchell, Lewin, and Lawler (1990) presented estimates in that volume that workers under incentive pay systems earn significantly higher wages, implying that these incentives may induce higher productivity.

In contrast to individual incentive effects, there is considerable evidence that group rewards are associated with productivity gains. Kruse

(1993) reviewed 26 econometric studies estimated across six nations. While each of these studies has statistical and methodological weaknesses, 57 percent of the 265 reported regression coefficients on profit-sharing variables had positive values statistically different from zero, and just 8.7 percent had negative values. Kruse's own results were consistent with average productivity gains of 2 to 5 percent. Another paper by Kruse (1992) reported weaker evidence in support of productivity gains resulting from the adoption of Employee Stock Option Plans (ESOPs). Kumbhakar and Dunbar (1993), however, estimated that ESOPs were associated with gains of approximately 2 percentage points per year.

A more recent review concluded that "Econometric evidence overwhelmingly favors the hypothesis that profit sharing enhances productivity" (Jones, Kato, and Pliskin 1997). This review finds little evidence, however, on how profit sharing enhances productivity. Still unknown are to what extent gains are due to greater worker effort, reduced absenteeism, or quits; adoption of different technologies; or enhanced worker participation.

The literature on compensation policies and productivity still is in its infancy. In general, no studies have tested for individual productivity effects of deferred compensation incentives.

INDIRECT EVIDENCE ON PENSIONS AND PRODUCTIVITY

This section reviews empirical evidence on patterns of pension coverage and the relationship between pension coverage and various labor market outcomes. We review and evaluate evidence that pension coverage is associated with higher wages, reduced quits and layoffs, and increased worker training, and that pension incentives affect retirement decisions. These relationships are indirect tests of the hypothesis that pensions raise productivity. While no single piece of indirect evidence is conclusive, a consistent pattern of results may be suggestive.

Pensions and Wages

Empirical studies of pension coverage patterns and the relation between pensions and labor market outcomes provide indirect evidence on the pension/productivity relationship. A robust finding that is consistent with pension-related productivity gains is the pension wage premium. If pensions are merely a vehicle for tax-preferred retirement saving, with no implications for employee productivity, there should be a trade-off between cash wages and pension compensation. On the other hand, if covered workers receive more training, put forth greater effort, or are less likely to continue working after their productivity has diminished, some of the resulting productivity gain should result in higher wages.[4]

The trade-off prediction is soundly rejected by the data. Even and Macpherson (1990) reported wage premiums of 15 percent for males and 13 percent for females, controlling for other characteristics, based on the May 1983 Current Population Survey. Gustman and Steinmeier (1995) also found significantly higher wages for pension-covered workers in the Survey of Income and Program Participation data. Allen and Clark (1987) estimated that average hourly earnings would be 38 percent higher in industries with 100 percent coverage, relative to having no pensions. Mitchell and Pozzebon (1987), using the 1983 Survey of Consumer Finances, also generally found a positive association between pension coverage and wages. Dorsey (1989) found pension wage premiums ranging from 12 to 29 percent based on wage regressions from four widely used data sets. Montgomery, Shaw, and Benedict (1992) found a negative pension coefficient; however, the coefficient was not always statistically significant and the estimated trade-off was less than dollar-for-dollar.[5]

The strength and durability of the wage/pension relationship across different data sets and empirical procedures supports the view that pensions enhance productivity. A complementary explanation is that the pension wage premium is itself an explicit incentive policy. Gustman and Steinmeier (1995) argued that pension premium represents an efficiency wage and that the latter is more important than pension backloading in reducing turnover. As discussed in Chapter 4, the pension penalty may be insufficient to deter shirking for workers with short tenure and so is coupled with an efficiency wage. This idea also suggests that the pension wage premium should fall as tenure grows and pension incentives become important. No direct test has been made of this prediction to date.

Do Pension Incentives Influence Turnover and Retirement?

The primary mechanism by which pensions raise productivity in both the specific training and monitoring models is by reducing turnover and inducing workers to retire earlier than otherwise. Thus an important body of indirect evidence is the effect of pension incentives on worker tenure and the age of retirement. Do workers actually respond to pension incentives?

The evidence that pension incentives affect retirement decisions is persuasive. Empirical studies of retirement behavior consistently have shown that workers with more generous pensions plans retire earlier and that retirement hazard functions fit the age pattern of pension benefit accruals; i.e., workers are more likely to retire when the present value of retirement benefits is highest.[6]

Empirical evidence on the effect of pensions on turnover is less clear. There is a consensus that turnover rates are lower in pension-covered jobs. Whether lower turnover is due to the pension tenure incentive is not settled, however. A recent study by Allen, Clark, and McDermed (1993) suggests that backloading of pension wealth in defined-benefit plans has important effects on turnover. Their results, based on the Panel Survey of Income Dynamics, attribute 40 percent of the difference in mobility between workers with and without pensions to defined-benefit backloading. The authors also found that the pension loss had a greater impact on layoffs than quits. Their results also indicated selectivity into pension-covered jobs, consistent with the view that deferred compensation attracts workers with favorable characteristics.

Gustman and Steinmeier (1995), in contrast, are skeptical that the pension capital loss is empirically important. They argue that pension tenure incentives are too small to have much impact, especially for younger workers. The typical loss in pension value for a quitting worker is about $17,000, which can be overcome by a pay gain of only about 3 percent per year at a new job over the remaining working life of a 35- to 44-year-old.

Of course, whether a loss of this magnitude is trivial is a matter of subjective judgement. Also, we have argued that a pension quit penalty that is greater than the value of the firm's investment is inefficient. An optimal employment does not deter all quits, only those which result in lower productivity. Thus the appropriate pension quit penalty depends upon the size of the firm's investment in workers.

Gustman and Steinmeier estimate turnover equations as a function of pension backloading but include a measure of current versus market alternative wages. They find that pension backloading explains a small portion of reduced mobility for covered workers once the control for the wage premium is introduced. The authors also estimate that defined-contribution plans have negative effects on turnover similar to those of defined-benefit pensions, a result confirmed by Even and Macpherson (1996). Since there is no capital loss in defined-contribution plans, this suggests that some other factor associated with pension coverage lowers mobility. The Gustman and Steinmeier results suggest that this other factor is an efficiency wage, presumably funded through higher productivity.

An explanation consistent with most of the empirical evidence is that deferred compensation associated with either type of pension attracts so-called "low discounters." We are not qualified to conduct a review of the literature of a branch of psychology, but there appears to be consensus that persons who are able to delay gratification experience substantially greater educational and career success.[7] Such individuals will be preferred by employers seeking long-term employees.[8] They should receive higher wages and also would have lower quit rates. Reduced quits follow if low discounters are more likely to receive firm-specific training, are inherently more stable, or if quitting a pension-covered job sends a signal that a worker is a high discounter (Ippolito, forthcoming).

Pensions and Layoffs

Two studies provide evidence that the pension separation penalty reduces employer-initiated separations (layoffs). Allen, Clark, and McDermed (1993), using the Panel Survey of Income Dynamics, found that pensions losses were a relatively greater deterrent to layoffs than quits. Similar results were reported by Cornwell, Dorsey, and

Mehrzad (1991) based upon the National Longitudinal Survey; workers facing average pension losses were about 5 percent less likely to be discharged than were uncovered workers. Reduced layoff probability is consistent with greater firm-specific training investments. This result also may reflect the deterrence of shirking by deferred compensation, as suggested by the principal-agent model, or self-selection of workers who are more productive and therefore less likely to forfeit deferred compensation due to a discharge.

Firms which provide defined-benefit pensions should try harder to avoid permanent layoffs, because they may signal opportunistic behavior to current and future employees. This reputation effect requires a productivity gain, however, since firms would not offer defined-benefit plans that constrain their ability to initiate layoffs unless there was an offsetting benefit.

Are Pension Penalties Flexible?

In the training model, the optimal quit penalty mirrors firm-specific productivity. Workers whose output unexpectedly declines should face a smaller quit penalty. If firm-specific productivity rents disappear altogether, there should be no incentive for continued tenure, and the ideal pension becomes fully portable. The separation penalty should be conditional on which party initiates the separation. If the firm initiates a layoff, no productive function is served by requiring that the worker who leaves involuntarily make a severance payment to the firm. A conditional pension loss could be created by indexing the preretirement wage of workers who are laid off but freezing the earnings of workers who quit. Pensions rules also could allow immediate vesting for workers who are laid off. A review of rules in major defined-benefit plans found no evidence that workers who were laid off were treated differently than quits (Doescher and Dorsey 1992).

Chapter 4 noted that a flexible separation penalty may not be feasible due to asymmetric information and moral hazard. Under some conditions, however, such incentive problems would be minimal. In the case of a plant closing or large layoff, shirking is not an issue, nor is there a concern that the firm would try to induce the entire work force to quit. Thus, waiving the pension loss in a mass layoff would not establish perverse incentives. Doescher and Dorsey found some evidence that employers attempted to offset pension losses for workers who were separated as part of a mass layoff or plant closing. Ad hoc early retirement offers are common under these circumstances.

Pension-covered workers also are more likely to have a formal severance payment plan, which automatically offsets separation losses. While formal severance programs cover less than half of all workers, informal severance payments are almost universal in plant closings.

Thus, defined-benefit separation penalties generally are independent of whether an employee quit or was discharged, but older workers who are part of a large layoff can expect significant benefit adjustments or severance payments. Given that workers nearing retirement face the largest separation losses, these informal benefits increase the flexibility of the separation penalty. Nevertheless, the penalty is not fully conditional on productivity, implying that unexpected declines in productivity can make the pension an impediment to efficient mobility.

Pensions, Training, and Productivity

Encouraging training investments in workers is one of the channels through which pension may promote productivity gains. There was little evidence, however, that pension-covered workers are more likely to receive training.[9] Results from two studies provide some indirect evidence that pensions complement specific training. A paper by Hutchens (1987) focused on the principal-agent model's prediction that deferred compensation and pensions are more likely to be found in jobs where monitoring employee effort is more costly. He assumed that jobs involving repetitive tasks are less costly to monitor. Estimates based on job characteristics from the Dictionary of Occupational Titles implied that workers in jobs classified as repetitive had a 9-percentage-point lower probability of pension coverage. This result is consistent with pensions as a deterrent to shirking, but it also has a training interpretation. Repetitive jobs likely require less training and, indeed, Hutchens reports a negative correlation between repetitive jobs and a DOT measure of time required to obtain the skills necessary to perform the job. More directly, the estimated coefficient on this training measure in the pension coverage equation is positive and empirically important.

Dorsey (1987) estimated the determinants of firms' decisions to sponsor primary defined-benefit versus defined-contribution coverage. Based on IRS-Form 5500 data, defined-benefit coverage was significantly less likely for firms in construction and in wholesale and retail trade, industries generally thought to require less firm-specific training relative to manufacturing. Also, firms in industries with high concentrations of professionals, managers, and craftsmen were more likely to sponsor defined-benefit pensions, and such coverage was associated with a lower rate of permanent layoff.

Defined-benefit plans also were more likely in large firms. This result is consistent with pensions as a complement to firm-specific training, under the Oi (1983) hypothesis that large firms' more rigid and formal production technologies necessitate greater investments in workers. Several other theories also predict this result. Monitoring costs may be greater in large firms, and there are economies of scale in administering defined-benefit plans (Mitchell and Andrews 1981). Large firms, whose survival probability is greater, also can more credibly promise future pension benefits.

The assumption that training does, in fact, raise productivity is generally accepted by academics and policymakers (Office of Technology Assessment 1990), but there is little direct evidence on the magnitude of the productivity gains. Early studies on this topic focused on whether wage-tenure profiles are consistent with the firm-specific training model. More recent studies generally conclude that training raises wages and that wage growth is faster after workers receive training (Lynch 1992). A few papers have tested the link between training and output, including Bishop (1990) and Holzer (1990). Bartel (1994) found that firms which support greater training expenditures experienced more rapid increases in productivity, and that training leads to higher performance reviews and faster wage growth (Bartel 1995).

THE DECLINE IN DEFINED-BENEFIT COVERAGE

The most important recent development in the pension market is the substantial loss of market share of defined-benefit plans. Table 2.2 showed that the percentage of workers having pensions with primary coverage under a defined-benefit plan fell from 87 percent to 57 percent between 1975 and 1992. Beyond the numbers, the changing pattern of pension coverage is suggested by the following quote from Edwin C. Hustead, a prominent benefit plan actuary and consultant:

> Back then . . . there was only one (retirement) plan. If you wanted to put in a savings plan, okay, but a defined benefit plan was the answer and we helped them choose one and put in that plan . . . Since the 1980s, however, employers have been hearing something like this. 'Well, there are two types of plans, there's a defined benefit plan and a defined contribution plan . . . On the defined benefit side, it's going to cost you $10,000 just to put that plan in place, and it's going to cost you $5,000 to $10,000 a year just to keep it going . . . So I would be glad to tell you about defined benefit plans, if you really want me to, but you don't want one, unless you have unusual circumstances, so let's install a defined contribution plan.' (Schmitt [1993], p. 161.)

Mr. Hustead's perception is reinforced by Internal Revenue Service records on requests for tax-qualified status for new retirement plans. In 1981, the IRS issued over 24,000 favorable determination letters for new defined-benefit plans and 58,000 for defined-contribution pensions. By 1992, fewer than 500 letters were issued approving new defined-benefit plans, compared with 14,000 new defined-contribution approvals (EBRI 1993).

Falling coverage raises questions about the economic justification for defined-benefit plans. Does the growing popularity of defined-contribution pensions imply that incentives for long tenure and early retirement are now less important? Has the demand for defined-benefit pensions declined because the value of long-term employment has diminished? The rapid growth of primary coverage by defined-contribution plans raises basic questions about the supply-side theory of pensions.

We believe that a careful examination of this trend suggests that it is largely policy-driven. The evidence does not support the view that the move to defined-contribution plans is motivated by the desire of firms and workers to avoid defined-benefit incentives. An alternative theory is that policy changes raised the relative cost and lowered the relative advantages of defined-benefit plans. This caused a shift in favor of defined-contribution plans by marginal sponsors, those for whom defined-benefit incentives were less valuable. Nevertheless, a large group of employees and sponsors continue to participate in defined-benefit plans. The latter are more likely to be large firms or in manufacturing, which arguably have a greater motivation for pension incentives.

A substantial portion of the growth in defined-contribution coverage reflects employment shifts away from sectors with traditionally high defined-benefit coverage. Gustman and Steinmeier (1992) estimated that at least half of the drop in defined-benefit share can be attributed to falling employment shares in large firms, in manufacturing industries, and in union membership. Clark and McDermed (1990) attribute a smaller, but still significant, share of the decline to employment shifts. An important factor in declining defined-benefit coverage is union membership. Ippolito (1995) used more recent union membership data and concluded that 55 percent of the coverage shift represented retrenchment in traditionally strong defined-benefit sectors.

Thus, perhaps half of the movement to defined-contribution plans represents a shift in choices. One could argue that this shift is an equilibrating adjustment as managers began to recognize the advantages of defined-contribution plans, but it is difficult to explain why it would take plan sponsors until the mid 1970s to reach this conclusion. This interpretation also leaves unexplained why, during the same time frame, the defined-benefit market share in Canada remained relatively constant. Between 1982 and 1992, defined-benefit coverage in Canada remained above 90 percent (Statistics Canada 1994).

Between 1979 and 1988, the overall percentage of pension-covered workers with primary defined-benefit plans fell by 12 percentage points.[10] The decline in defined-benefit coverage occurred primarily in large firms in manufacturing industries. Table 5.1 disaggregates the change in primary defined-benefit coverage by size of employer.[11] It shows that the growth in defined-contribution coverage was greatest among small plans. The percentage of covered workers who had defined-benefit coverage fell 15.5 percentage points for firms with 200–499 employees, but the decline was only 3.5 points for firms with more than 5,000 employees. Note that the share of total pension coverage, by either type of plan, accounted for by smaller plans rose, reinforcing the overall trend to defined-contribution coverage. Firms with

Table 5.1 Primary Defined-Benefit Coverage by Firm Size, 1979–1988

Employees	Covered workers in D-B plans, 1979 (%)	Change in covered workers in D-B plans 1979-88 (%)	Change in total pension share[a] (%)
<200	59.9	−11.4	2.4
200–499	62.6	−15.5	2.6
500–999	69.9	−11.0	1.3
1,000–1,999	77.7	− 8.3	1.3
2,000–4,999	81.8	− 6.8	0.3
5,000 +	90.0	− 3.5	−8.1

SOURCE: Ippolito (1995).
[a]Pension share is the percentage of total coverage accounted for by each firm size category.

5,000 or more employees lost 8.1 percentage points of the total pension market.[12]

Table 5.2 provides additional evidence that the trend to defined-contribution primary coverage is largely due to small firms. Between 1985 and 1989, the greatest losses in the number of defined-benefit plans and participants were in plans with fewer than 50 participants. The percentage of primary coverage plans which were defined-benefit fell by 31 points among small sponsors over this period. The decline in participants by firm size is similar. Among large plans, the number of defined-benefit plans and covered workers remained stable.

Coverage trends also differ by industry. Table 5.3 suggests that industries which initially had high defined-benefit coverage were less likely to adopt defined-contribution plans. The coverage rate remained high in manufacturing, but construction, services, and wholesale trade, which were less likely to have defined-benefit coverage initially, experienced high growth in primary defined-contribution coverage. Again, industries with larger declines in defined-benefit coverage also saw their share of total pension coverage shrink.

Growth in primary coverage by defined-contribution plans thus largely reflects adoptions by small firms and in nonmanufacturing industries, coupled with a rising share of total pension coverage in these sectors. Arguably, the value of supply-side incentives of defined-benefit pensions is less in sectors where defined-contribution coverage

Table 5.2   Changes in Primary Defined-Benefit Plans and Coverage, 1985–1989

Participants	Change in plans (%)	Change in participants (%)	Distribution of participants, 1989 (%)
2-49	−31.0	−29.3	3.1
50–249	−22.6	−22.8	6.6
250–499	−13.9	−13.4	5.2
500–999	−14.2	−14.0	7.0
1,000–2,499	− 5.9	− 5.6	12.6
2,500–4,999	− 1.7	0.3	10.8
5,000+	1.6	0.2	54.7

SOURCE: EBRI (1993) tabulations from Form 5500 reports.

Table 5.3   Primary Defined-Benefit Coverage By Industry, 1979–1988

Employees	Pension covered workers in D-B plans, 1979 (%)	Change in covered workers in D-B plans, 1979–88 (%)	Change in total pension share[a] (%)
Manufacturing	90.7	−3.5	−3.9
Transportation	90.0	−3.7	−1.0
Public admin.	86.3	−1.3	0.6
Finance	85.5	−7.2	−0.3
Mining	79.8	−4.9	0.2
Services	79.8	−12.2	3.8
Agriculture	78.8	−5.9	0.1
Wholesale trade	66.6	−9.4	0.6
Retail trade	64.5	−6.7	0.6
Construction	32.3	−12.7	0.2

SOURCE: Ippolito (1995).
[a]Pension share is the percentage of total coverage accounted for by each firm size category.

has been growing most rapidly. Training requirements, in general, are lower for nonmanufacturing employees. Monitoring costs also should be less in small firms, reducing the importance of deferred compensation arrangements. Defined-benefit among these employers initially was lower, consistent with this conjecture (Dorsey 1987). This suggests that the decline in defined-benefit coverage largely has occurred at the margin. A number of policy changes have raised the relative cost and lowered the benefits of defined-benefit plans.

Federal regulation of defined-benefit pensions expanded significantly with the adoption of ERISA in the mid 1970s. Chapter 2 presented a brief overview of reporting, vesting, funding, and insurance standards. Nondiscrimination rules also became increasingly strict and complex (Utgoff 1991). These regulations raised administrative costs for all pensions, but relatively more for defined-benefit plans. A widely cited study for the PBGC by the Hay-Huggins Company (1990) estimated that the administration cost per participant rose 180 and 97 percent for defined-benefit and defined-contribution plans, respectively, between 1981 and 1991. While the ratio of defined-contribution to defined-benefit administration costs fell for plans of all size, the effect was greater for small plans. Tax preferences were trimmed for pension compensation over this period, as well. Again, the greatest impact was on defined-benefit plans (EBRI 1993).[13]

Ippolito (1995) argues that regulatory cost can be only a partial explanation, since the administrative cost differential increased significantly only for smaller plan sponsors. He calculates that the difference in costs grew to 13 percent of the average pension contribution for plans with fewer than 15 participants by 1991. However, for the largest plans the differential still was less than 1 percent of contributions.

Higher administrative costs help to explain the shift to defined-contribution plans by smaller firms. They cannot explain the more modest but important movement to the defined-contribution format by sponsors of large plans. Table 5.1 shows that defined-contribution share grew among firms with more than 1,000 employees. Ippolito attributes most of this trend to the authorization in 1981 of the 401(k) plan. This allowed, for the first time, employees to make voluntary, pre-tax contributions to a defined-contribution fund. Employers are permitted to match these contributions up to a limit. The 401(k) plan was warmly received in the pension market, becoming the primary coverage vehicle for 12 percent of covered workers by 1988.

A conjecture is that productive incentives have been a factor in 401(k) growth among large firms. Like other pension plans, they attract workers who value deferred compensation. We have suggested that firms would prefer to hire workers who are able to delay gratification, the so-called "low discounters." Defined-contribution plans perform this task more efficiently because the availability of lump-sum distributions provides an incentive for high discounters to quit. A further advantage of 401(k) pensions is matching, which allows firms to pay a compensation premium to workers who make high voluntary contributions. Ippolito estimated that 70 percent of the increase in preference for 401(k) pensions, between 1979 and 1988, came from firms that likely would otherwise have chosen defined-benefit plans.

401(k) plans do not reward long tenure. However, the ability to target higher compensation to workers who are more forward-looking may reduce turnover. We also have heard arguments that providing any type of coverage as a type of efficiency wage is a more effective tool for discouraging quits than deferred compensation. Evidence that quit rates are lower under either type of pension plan suggests that 401(k) incentives are a good substitute for deferred compensation.

Defined-contribution plans are at a distinct disadvantage, however, at subsidizing early retirement. Anecdotal evidence indicates that retirement incentives remain valuable, especially in large firms. The growth of 401(k) coverage seems likely to continue to displace defined-benefit coverage, but predicting the ultimate outcome requires a better understanding than we now have of the value of early retirement incentives.

We conclude that the trend to defined-contribution pensions is not conclusive evidence that defined-benefit incentives have outlived their usefulness. Much of the trend reflects employment growth in sectors which traditionally have favored the defined-contribution format. Changes in coverage rates account for perhaps half of the decline in defined-benefit coverage. The latter, which are most evident in small, nonmanufacturing firms, likely have been driven by policy changes which increased the relative cost of administering and lowered the demand for defined-benefit plans. Defined-benefit coverage remains a factor in large, manufacturing firms, where the gains from long-term employment contracts arguably are greater.

SUMMARY

There is little direct evidence that workers or firms with pensions are more productive. Indirect evidence, however, is consistent with a productivity role for pensions. In particular, there is robust evidence that pension coverage is associated with large wage premiums. Pension-covered workers also experience lower quit and layoff rates and are more likely to receive training.

While there are clear differences in outcomes between workers in jobs that provide pensions and those that do not, the mechanism which drives these results is not known. The differences are consistent with a separation penalty which discourages shirking or promotes firm-specific training. But there is evidence that defined-contribution coverage also is associated with favorable labor market outcomes. An hypothesis consistent with the latter is that pensions attract workers who are inherently more forward-looking and presumably better employees. There is little evidence to judge whether and to what extent productivity gains result from each of these incentive channels.

An argument that defined-benefit incentives enhance productivity has been the very fact of their popularity, but the recent surge of primary defined-contribution coverage calls into question the productivity advantages of defined-benefit pensions. Our analysis suggests that the trend does not deny the relevance of the productivity theory. Much of the movement towards defined-contribution plans reflects structural employment shifts or policy changes that caused marginal sponsors to switch from defined-benefit plans. Changes in pension coverage were much less evident among large, manufacturing establishments, where gains from long-term employment likely are greatest.

There are indications that 401(k) plans are substituting for defined-benefit plans among large employers. The ability to target wage premiums to forward-looking employees may be a good substitute for defined-benefit tenure incentives. If so, the remaining productive advantage of traditional defined-benefit plans is early retirement incentives.

NOTES

1. Another theory is that employers preferred delayed vesting to reduce pension costs. The longer that workers waited to become vested, the lower the costs of the plan due to quits and layoffs. However, this theory suggests that employers were getting something for nothing. If workers were aware of the low likelihood of receiving benefits, they would place low value on the pension. Employers would have to pay higher current wages, then, to provide a competitive compensation package.

2. It is possible that retirement incentives are valuable but rewarding long tenure is not. Productivity may decline with age, even if there is no firm-specific component. However, the human capital model does suggest the possibility that firm-specific skills will depreciate and therefore retirement incentives will be more valuable in jobs that require training. Retirement incentives also are more likely if deferred compensation deters shirking.

3. The efficiency wage hypothesis also implies that paying higher wages will increase labor productivity, implying small employment reductions for firms paying higher wages. To the extent that the wage elasticity estimated by Kruse measures this effect, the pension/productivity effect would be understated.

4. Note that some of this rent will in fact be a compensating wage premium to offset the cost of reduced mobility and flexibility.

5. It should be noted that single-equation estimates may be biased upward. Pension coverage is a choice variable and cannot be treated as exogenous in a wage regression. The potential for bias arises because an important factor in the pension decision is taxable income. It may be that the OLS pension coefficients partly reflect a greater preference for pension tax incentives by high-wage workers. While no published estimates have attempted to estimate the wage-pension trade-off with endogenous pension coverage, Dorsey's results (1989) suggested that a strong positive correlation between pension coverage and wages remains after controlling for selectivity.

6. For example, Fields and Mitchell (1984) and Stock and Wise (1990). Also, see the review of retirement models in Quinn, Burkhauser, and Myers (1990).

7. A well-publicized experiment involved giving 4-year-olds a choice of a small reward (for example, one marshmallow) immediately or a higher reward later. Pre-schoolers who were able to delay gratification averaged considerably higher SAT scores and were rated higher by parents in the ability to concentrate and cope with stress (Mischel, Shoda, and Rodriguez 1989).

8. The difference between a low and a high discounter can be illustrated by two bumper stickers we recently have seen: "Hard Work Has a Future Payoff. Laziness Pays Off NOW!" and "Warning: Dates in Calendar Are Closer Than They

Appear." Essentially, this theory states that employers would prefer to hire people whose cars sported the latter.

9. We present new tests of this hypothesis in Chapter 6.

10. The decline in defined-benefit coverage shown in these tables is less than that reported for the universe of plans, primarily reflecting the exclusion of plans with fewer than 100 participants from the analysis.

11. These estimates are taken from Ippolito's (1995) analysis of IRS Form 5500 reports for 1979 and 1988.

12. In 1979, 69.7 percent of all workers with pensions were in firms with 5,000 or more employees. By 1988, this share had fallen to (69.7 − 8.1) = 61.6 percent.

13. For example, the 150 percent funding maximum established in 1987, which effectively prohibited sponsors of plans with younger employees to fully fund future liabilities at the pre-tax rate of return.

6 Estimates of the Pension/Training Relationship

An important conclusion of the previous chapter was that there is little formal empirical evidence that pensions promote higher productivity. The remainder of this monograph presents new empirical results on the relationship between pension coverage and productivity. This chapter tests one of the channels by which pensions may raise workforce productivity: by complementing training investments in workers.

No study has tested directly the prediction that employers who provide training will compensate workers with pensions in order to discourage quits. While there are several studies of the empirical determinants of pension coverage,[1] and others which have identified factors encouraging the provision of employer-provided training,[2] only a few have tested the relationship between these two employment outcomes. Papers by Hutchens (1987) and Dorsey (1987), reviewed in the previous chapter, provided indirect evidence of a positive relationship between pensions and training. More recently, Johnson (1996) used the National Longitudinal Survey of Mature Men to find that retirees who reported more job training received higher pension income. His empirical model, however, was not based upon a model of pension career incentives.[3]

We test for a relationship between pensions and training with two data sets: the matched 1991 Current Population Survey (CPS) files and the 1992 Health and Retirement Survey. The results are consistent with a productivity role for pensions. Controlling for other worker and firm characteristics, we estimate a positive and significant correlation between pension coverage and training. Workers who receive training also are slightly more likely to participate in a defined-benefit plan, given that they have a pension.

THE INCENTIVE MODEL OF PENSIONS AND TRAINING

The specific training model predicts that workers who receive training also will be provided with incentives to discourage quits. Chapter 4 presented a view of the pension quit penalty as such a severance tax. The training model also predicts that wages will be less flexible downward and that productivity will diminish more sharply as workers age. The optimal contract thus includes a severance payment, which also may be provided by a defined-benefit pension.

Pensions also attract workers who are more forward-looking. This incentive also should encourage training, as persons with low discount rates value future wage gains more highly and hence are more willing to undergo training investments. The quit penalty and retirement incentive suggests that training should be related only to defined-benefit coverage. Self-selection of workers by internal discount rates also is achieved by defined-contribution pensions, as we have seen.

ESTIMATION PROCEDURE

The hypothesis tested in this chapter is quite straightforward: workers who receive training are more likely to be covered by a pension. Of course, each of these variables is an endogenous outcome of worker and firm choices. Given its decision to train, employers are more likely to include a defined-benefit pension in the compensation package. At the same time, the willingness of employees to accept the constraints of pension career incentives influences the training decision. Ideally, we would estimate a model of jointly determined pension coverage and training:

Eq. 6.1 $P = P[X,Z,T]$

Eq. 6.2 $T = T[Y,V,P]$,

where $P =$ a pension coverage dummy variable;

$T =$ a dummy variable indicating training received at the workplace;

$X =$ worker attributes associated with higher demand for
pension coverage;

$Z =$ firm attributes associated with greater willingness to
provide pension coverage;

$Y =$ worker attributes associated with greater productivity
gains from training; and

$V =$ firm attributes associated with greater productivity
gains from training.

Previous studies separately have estimated equations similar to Eqs. 6.1 and 6.2, and they have found that both pension coverage and training likelihood are affected by education, age, gender, job tenure, marital status, union membership, and wage income. Firm size and industry also affect both employment outcomes. Thus the data available to us preclude identifying restrictions sufficient to estimate structural parameters from Eqs. 6.1 and 6.2. It is not possible to exclude, *a priori* or empirically, any of the variables in the X and Z vectors from either the training or the pension equation.

However, identifying which causal effect is greatest goes beyond our more modest goal of testing for pensions and training complementarity. A finding of zero correlation or a negative correlation between these two employment outcomes is sufficient to reject the prediction that pension incentives are related to training and, ultimately, to productivity gains. Therefore, our basic empirical model is a single-stage pension coverage equation, with training variables included among the set of regressors. But we emphasize that the coefficient on the training variable is a reduced-form estimate of correlation between pension coverage and training, controlling for other pension coverage (and training) determinants. We do not mean to imply that causation runs only from training to pension coverage.

CPS DATA

Until recently, no data set would have allowed a test of even the simple prediction that pension and training are complements. Most training surveys did not include pension compensation. The January 1991

CPS has a detailed job training supplemental questionnaire but no information on pension coverage. Fortunately, we were able to use a matching procedure to obtain information on respondents' pension status from the March CPS. Half of the January rotation groups were surveyed in March, including questions about pension coverage and firm size at the main job during 1990. Another match to the March and April CPS brought in a union status variable. The completed matched file is a sample of more than 11,000 full-time, private-sector employees.

This data set has several advantages. First, coverage is more representative of the overall labor force, with all age groups and both sexes included. Other training surveys have focused on younger males or oversampled low-wage workers (Brown 1990). Second, it includes information on employer size, which is an important control for both training (Oi 1983) and pension coverage (Mitchell and Andrews 1981). Finally, the CPS training questions provide information on type and place of training. Each employed respondent was asked, "Since you obtained your present job, did you take any training to improve your skills?" To those answering "yes," additional questions were put concerning type of training, including reading, writing, and math skills, computer or other technical instruction, or managerial training. They also were asked where their training took place—in school, at the company's training facility, or through informal on-the-job training (OJT). These additional prompts allow a test of whether training that is likely to be more firm-specific has a stronger correlation with pension coverage than general training.

An important drawback is that the pension variable does not distinguish between defined-benefit and defined-contribution coverage. We addressed this problem analyzing data from the 1992 Health and Retirement Survey, which includes information about pension plan type as well as a training measure.

We restricted the sample to private-sector, non-self-employed persons, age 20–65, who reported usually working at least 35 hours per week. Table 6.1 presents sample means and standard deviations. Forty-five percent reported receiving training at their current job, including 20.4 percent receiving formal training at the job, 18 percent informal OJT, and 12.9 percent training in an outside classroom. These figures generally are consistent with estimates from other surveys.[4]

Table 6.1 Means and Standard Deviations[a]

Variable	Mean	Standard deviation
Training at current job	0.453	0.498
Training by place		
At company, formal classroom	0.204	0.403
At company, informal OJT	0.180	0.385
Outside company, classroom	0.129	0.336
Training by type		
Reading, writing, math	0.062	0.242
Computer-related	0.161	0.367
Other occupation-specific technical skills	0.289	0.453
Managerial	0.136	0.343
Pension	0.548	0.498
Years of education	13.1	2.56
Years of tenure	7.85	7.82
Female	0.434	0.496
Nonwhite	0.116	0.320
Age	38.3	10.8
Married, spouse present	0.641	0.480
Firm size (no. of employees)		
25–99	0.151	0.358
100–499	0.176	0.381
500–999	0.710	0.256
1,000+	0.411	0.492
Union member	0.160	0.366

[a]Sample size = 11,269 observations.

Training also can be decomposed by type. Just 6 percent reported training in general skills (reading and mathematics), while 16 percent reported computer training. Training in "other occupation-specific skills" was received by 29 percent, and 13.6 percent participated in programs aimed at developing managerial or supervisory skills. The percentage of workers participating in an employer-sponsored pension plan was 54.8, which is in the range of other reported CPS coverage estimates for full-time, private-sector employees.

CPS ESTIMATES

Results from probit estimates of several specifications of the pension coverage equation are reported in Table 6.2. The coefficient on the training variable is positive and significant in each model. The probit coefficient of 0.427 in column **a** implies a partial derivative of 0.169; that is, before controlling for other determinants of pension coverage, workers who report receiving training at their current job are 16.9 percent more likely to have a pension.

Column **b** introduces several control variables suggested by theory and previous empirical studies of pension coverage. These include age and income (Dorsey 1982), gender (Even and Macpherson 1990), firm size (Parsons 1992), and union status (Freeman 1985). These studies controlled for education, possibly as a proxy for the employee's discount rate, because those who invest more in education demonstrate a willingness to defer income. Previous studies have found that married workers are more likely to have pension coverage. This result may reflect higher marginal tax rates in marriage, or that married workers have greater job stability and thus value nonportable pension benefits more than workers who have shorter expected tenure.

The coefficient estimates on these controls reported in column **b** are consistent with earlier studies. Annual wage income, education, age, employment at a larger firm, being married, and union membership each increase the likelihood of having a pension. More importantly, even after adding these controls, we estimate that workers with training are nearly 7 percent more likely to have a pension.

It is noteworthy that the training coefficient remains positive after controlling for annual wage income. Part of the simple correlation between pension coverage and training likely reflects preferences for tax-preferred pension compensation by higher-wage employees. Another hypothesis for the correlation between training and pension coverage is offered by Gustman and Steinmeier (1995). They argue that pension coverage is part of an efficiency wage package, where the latter is more important in reducing quits than pension incentives. Both of these ideas are reasons why it is important to include wage income in the model. Indeed, when the income variable is excluded, the estimated training coefficient is substantially larger (column **c**).

Table 6.2 Probit Pension Coverage Estimates[a]

Variable	a	b	c	d
Intercept	−0.069	−4.326	−3.822	−11.17
	(4.32)	(22.83)	(21.19)	(27.24)
TRAINING AT CURRENT JOB	0.427	0.170	0.266	0.111
	(17.78)	(6.09)	(9.87)	(3.68)
	0.169	0.067	0.105	0.044
EDUCATION		0.022	0.070	−0.010
		(3.78)	(12.92)	(1.42)
		0.009	0.028	−0.004
MARRIED, SPOUSE PRESENT		0.130	0.185	0.084
		(4.54)	(6.61)	(2.75)
		0.051	0.073	0.033
AGE		0.046	0.082	0.024
		(4.54)	(9.43)	(2.39)
		0.051	0.033	0.009
AGE SQUARED		−0.0004	−0.0008	−0.0002
		(3.79)	(7.47)	(1.54)
		−0.0002	-0.0003	−0.0001
FEMALE		0.020	−0.212	0.165
		(0.69)	(7.96)	(4.84)
		0.008	−0.084	0.065

(continued)

Table 6.2 (continued)

Variable	a	b	c	d
FIRM SIZE:				
25–99		0.575	0.615	0.519
		(12.48)	(13.68)	(10.65)
		0.227	0.243	0.205
100–499		0.851	0.919	0.771
		(19.23)	(21.23)	(16.37)
		0.336	0.363	0.305
500–999		1.041	1.149	0.935
		(17.87)	(20.13)	(14.98)
		0.411	0.454	0.370
1000+		1.308	1.405	1.186
		(33.10)	(36.52)	(27.81)
		0.517	0.555	0.469
UNION MEMBER		0.439	0.494	0.400
		(11.25)	(12.92)	(9.57)
		0.173	0.195	0.157
LN(ANNUALWAGE INCOME)		0.608		
		(23.90)		
		0.240		
PREDICTED ANNUAL INCOME				0.983
				(20.52)
				0.390

[a]The top row for each variable is the probit coefficient, while the bottom row is the partial derivative evaluated at the sample mean of the independent variable. It represents how a one-unit change in the independent variable changes the predicted probability of pension coverage. The absolute value of the t-statistic for the probit coefficient is in parentheses. Sample size = 11,269 observations.

Nevertheless, the likelihood of pension coverage is greater for trained workers, independent of higher wages.

A problem with including wage income as a regressor is the endogeneity of pension coverage and wages. While more highly compensated employees have a higher tax-induced demand for pension coverage, to the extent that other variables control for the worker's total compensation, theory predicts a trade-off between any nonwage benefit and current wages. That is, a higher likelihood of pension coverage should result in lower current wages, and the sign of the income coefficient is ambiguous. We have explored the latter issue elsewhere (Dorsey 1982).

Our concern here is whether or not the training coefficient is sensitive to the endogeneity of wage income. Column **d** reports estimates of the model when actual wage income is replaced with an instrumental variable, predicted annual wage income.[5] The larger coefficient on the instrument compared to actual income is consistent with findings in a previous study (Dorsey 1982). The training coefficient declines when the income instrument is used, but it still is positive and statistically significant.

The positive training estimate also is robust to specifications that control for industry and occupation. Table 6.3 lists estimates obtained from the pension coverage model but with the addition of 5 industry and 11 occupation dummy variables. Not surprisingly, the estimate of the training coefficient is smaller, but again, it reveals a positive relationship.

These results leave little doubt that there is an empirical link between pension coverage and training. This is evidence consistent with the incentive function of pensions, especially given the controls for income and other worker and firm characteristics. There are other interpretations of the correlation between pensions and training, however, such as pensions as an efficiency wage or other variants of a "good jobs-bad jobs" view of the labor market. The rest of this chapter presents further tests of the incentive theory of pensions and training. First, we examine the relationship between pension coverage and different types of training. Second, we ask whether training increases the likelihood of defined-benefit as opposed to defined-contribution pension coverage.

Table 6.3 Probit Pension Coverage Estimates with Industry and Occupation Controls[a]

Variable	a	b
Intercept	−1.266	−1.499
	(7.43)	(19.35)
TRAINING AT CURRENT JOB	0.082	0.057
	(7.43)	(5.04)
EDUCATION	0.022	0.009
	(7.97)	(3.29)
MARRIED, SPOUSE PRESENT	0.060	0.046
	(5.35)	(4.01)
AGE	0.030	0.018
	(8.53)	(4.96)
AGE SQUARED	−0.0007	−0.0001
	(6.75)	(3.69)
FEMALE	−0.086	−0.005
	(7.27)	(0.36)
FIRM SIZE		
25–99	0.222	0.211
	(12.16)	(11.45)
100–499	0.329	0.306
	(18.64)	(17.05)
500–999	0.420	0.382
	(18.21)	(16.31)
1000+	0.533	0.499
	(33.25)	(30.44)
UNION MEMBER	0.197	0.169
	(12.36)	(10.46)
LN(ANNUALWAGE INCOME)		0.223
		(21.14)
OCCUPATION		
MANAGER/PROFESSIONAL	0.075	−0.013
	(3.78)	(0.65)
TECHNICAL/SALES	0.058	0.017
	(3.19)	(0.93)

Variable	a	b
SERVICE	−0.097	−0.071
	(3.88)	(2.81)
FARMING/FORESTRY	−0.052	−0.023
	(0.65)	(0.27)
PRECISION/CRAFT	0.029	−0.003
	(1.47)	(0.13)
INDUSTRY		
Agriculture	−0.241	−0.228
	(3.00)	(2.76)
Mining	0.038	−0.006
	(0.79)	(0.12)
Construction	−0.128	−0.144
	(4.31)	(4.78)
Durable manufacturing	−0.003	−0.010
	(0.19)	(0.50)
Transport/Utilities	−0.062	−0.080
	(2.55)	(3.21)
Wholesale trade	−0.064	−0.077
	(2.29)	(2.71)
Retail trade	−0.216	−0.181
	(10.01)	(8.18)
Banking/Insurance	−0.030	−0.027
	(1.26)	(1.09)
Business services	−0.148	−0.142
	(5.44)	(5.10)
Personal services	−0.324	−0.294
	(8.21)	(7.30)
Entertainment	−0.241	−0.222
	(4.08)	(3.66)
Professional services	−0.072	−0.047
	(3.37)	(2.11)

[a]For brevity, we do not report the probit coefficients in this table. The estimates shown are the partial derivatives of the independent variable, evaluated at the mean of the independent variables, and the absolute value of the t-statistics (in parentheses). The excluded occupational group is operators/laborer, while the excluded industry is nondurable manufacturing.

GENERAL VS. SPECIFIC TRAINING

The prediction that employers use pensions to discourage quits of trained workers applies primarily to firm-specific training. Human capital theory predicts that the costs of general training, skills which are easily transferable to other firms, will be borne by the worker. If training is completely general, the firm will not invest in its employees and will be unconcerned about quits. The quit penalty makes sense only when the firm invests in its workers, i.e., when training is firm-specific. Testing this implication is difficult, unfortunately, because a clean distinction between general and specific training is not available in this, or any other, survey of training.

However, the type and location categories of training reported in Table 6.1 should reflect differences in the transferability of skills. Reading, math, writing, and computer-related training arguably are easily transferred across firms. Managerial and supervisory skills also would seem to be highly portable. On the other hand, workers who have received firm-specific training would be most likely to report this as "other technical skills specific to the occupation."[6] The location of training also may reflect differences in specificity. Programs at an outside classroom suggest general skills, while informal OJT is more likely to focus on firm-specific needs.

If these categorizations are accurate, workers' responses should be consistent by type and place. Table 6.4 lists Pearson correlation coefficients between training place and type for all workers who reported receiving some training. As expected, the weakest correlation for the occupation-specific category is with training outside the firm. We also expected to find that the strongest correlation for informal OJT would be with occupation-specific training, and the weakest with reading, math, and writing skills. While these categories are clearly imperfect, they should be a useful proxy.

We tested the specific-training hypothesis by replacing the single training variable with a set of dummy variables for type and place of training. We expect that occupation-specific training and informal OJT will have larger coefficients in the pension coverage model than other training categories. Table 6.5 reports coefficient estimates for each of the training categories.[7] The results for type of training are mixed. An

Table 6.4 Pearson Correlation Coefficients for Training by Type and Place

Training	Reading, math, etc.	Computer	Managerial	Occupation-specific
Outside school	0.191	0.131	0.073	0.013
Company classroom	0.067	0.175	0.201	0.067
Informal OJT	0.020	0.052	0.001	0.070

expected result is that workers who received training in basic language and math or managerial skills—general training—were not significantly more likely than untrained workers to have a pension. Occupation-specific training, in contrast, is positively related to pension coverage. However, the largest coefficient is for computer training, which we judge to be quite general.

Column **b** shows the results when training is broken out by place. The coefficient on formal company training is larger than that for training received outside the firm. However, the place of training most likely to convey nontransferable skills, informal OJT, has the weakest relationship with training.

HEALTH AND RETIREMENT SURVEY

A more powerful test of the incentive theory of pensions can be made by distinguishing between defined-benefit and defined-contribution coverage. If the explanation for the positive relationship between pensions and training is tenure and retirement incentives, training should be associated with a greater likelihood of defined-benefit coverage. Unfortunately, the March CPS pension data does not distinguish coverage by plan type. Information on type of coverage is available in the pension supplement to the May 1988 CPS, but this file cannot be matched to the 1991 CPS training supplement.

Given the lack of direct information on plan type in the 1991 CPS surveys, we have employed the 1992 Health and Retirement Survey (HRS) to examine the impact of training on the defined-benefit/defined-contribution decision. An important advantage of the HRS is

Table 6.5 Pension Coverage Model with Controls for Place and Type of Training[a]

	a	b
Training by type		
Reading, math, etc.	0.093	
	(1.52)	
	0.037	
Computer	0.201	
	(4.93)	
	0.080	
Managerial	0.042	
	(0.96)	
	0.017	
Occupation-specific	0.136	
	(4.36)	
	0.054	
Other	−0.022	
	(0.41)	
	−0.009	
Training by place		
Outside company, classroom		0.099
		(2.39)
		0.039
At company, formal		0.245
		(6.88)
		0.097
At company, informal		0.052
		(1.45)
		0.020
Other		0.096
		(1.77)
		0.038

[a]These pension coverage models also include as regressors years of education, gender, marital status, firm size, age and age-squared, union membership, and annual wage income. The specification is identical to that for equation a (column **a** in Table 6.3) but with the expanded training variables. The top row for each variable is the probit coefficient, while the bottom row is the partial derivative evaluated at the sample mean of the independent variable. It represents how a one-unit change in the independent variable changes the predicted probability of pension coverage. The absolute value of the t-statistic for the probit coefficient is in parentheses. Sample size = 11,269 observations.

that it includes information on pension plan type as well as a measure of training (the respondent's opinion regarding the number of years of experience beyond formal schooling to achieve proficiency in her job).

For the analysis, we restricted the HRS sample to wage and salary workers, aged 51–61, who reported usually working at least 35 hours per week. In order to exclude as many public-sector workers as possible, we also deleted workers in the public administration industry (unlike the CPS, there is no public-sector status variable in the HRS). Thus the HRS sample restrictions are the same as the CPS restrictions, except for the incomplete exclusion of public-sector workers. The sample consists of 3,990 employees.

Table 6.6 reports estimates of the determinants of two models of pensions: 1) pension coverage, and 2) defined-benefit coverage, given that the worker has a pension. The first column reports the pension coverage equation results for comparison with the previously reported CPS-based findings. The coefficient estimates on the control variables are consistent. Education, employment at a larger establishment, being married, and union membership each increase the likelihood of being covered by a pension. Most importantly, we estimate that workers with the mean years of training (3.56 years) are 7 percent more likely to have a pension than workers with no training. This is virtually identical to our finding in the CPS data.

The second column reports estimates of the type of coverage for a sample restricted to workers who have a pension. The dependent variable is equal to unity if workers reported primary coverage under a defined-benefit pension plan; zero, if coverage was defined-contribution.

The results indicate that union members and employees of large establishments are more likely to be covered under a defined-benefit plan. These results are consistent with previous estimates of the determinants of plan type (Dorsey 1987). For our purposes, the most consequential result is the positive coefficient on the training variable. From the quadratic form of the model, we estimated that the mean years of training increases the probability of defined-benefit coverage by 2.3 percentage points compared to workers without training. The coefficient estimate is significant at the 10 percent confidence level.

This confirms the results reported in Dorsey and Macpherson (1997), who constructed a measure of predicted training using 1993

Table 6.6 Training and Pension Coverage and Defined Benefit Coverage Using Health and Retirement Survey Data[a]

Variable	Pension coverage[b]	Defined-benefit coverage[c]
Intercept	−1.083	16.186
	(0.13)	(1.75)
	−0.337	5.91
YEARS OF TRAINING	0.074	0 .021
	(6.55)	(1.65)
	0.023	0.008
YEARS OF TRAINING SQUARED	−0.003	−0.001
	(6.33)	(1.77)
	−0.001	−0.0004
YEARS OF EDUCATION	0.093	0.049
	(11.09)	(4.95)
	0.029	0.018
MARRIED, SPOUSE PRESENT	0.229	0.116
	(4.17)	(1.86)
	0.071	0.042
PLANT SIZE:		
5–14	0.280	0.027
	(2.74)	(0.17)
	0.087	0.010
15–24	0.525	0.003
	(4.58)	(0.01)
	0.163	0.001
25–99	0.769	0.076
	(7.92)	(0.51)
	0.239	0.028
100–499	1.128	0.191
	(11.33)	(1.29)
	0.350	0.070
500+	1.519	0.376
	(14.34)	(2.53)
	0.472	0.137

Variable	Pension coverage[b]	Defined-benefit coverage[c]
UNION MEMBER	0.883	0.784
	(14.27)	(13.97)
	0.274	0.286
AGE	−0.021	−0.615
	(0.07)	(1.85)
	−0.007	−0.225
AGE SQUARED/100	0.011	0.553
	(0.11)	(1.86)
	0.003	0.202
FEMALE	−0.006	0.070
	(0.11)	(1.24)
	−0.002	0.025
Sample size	3,990	2,748

[a]The top row for each variable is the probit coefficient, while the bottom row is the partial derivative evaluated at the sample mean of the independent variable. It represents how a one-unit change in the independent variable changes the predicted probability of pension coverage. The absolute value of the t-statistic for the probit coefficient is in parentheses.
[b]The dependent variable is equal to 1 if covered by a pension and zero otherwise.
[c]The dependent variable is equal to 1 if primary pension coverage is by a defined-benefit plan, and zero if by defined-contribution plan.

CPS data and then estimated that this instrument raised the probability of defined-benefit coverage. These results, however, were sensitive to the variables used to identify the training equation.

This finding is important, because while the pension/training correlation is robust, several theories are capable of explaining this result. The relationship between training and defined-benefit coverage, however, is a more discriminating test. If training was associated with proportionately higher defined-contribution and defined-benefit coverage, we could reject the hypothesis that tenure and retirement incentives were reasons for the correlation. None of the alternative theories easily can explain why workers with training should prefer defined-benefit coverage. The relationship is statistically significant but relatively weak. Defined-benefit coverage appears to be related to training, but the latter is less important than firm size or union status.

SUMMARY

This chapter has tested one of the channels through which pensions raise productivity: encouraging training investments. There is a clear empirical connection between pension coverage and job training. While data limitations do not allows us to identify causation between these two endogenous variables, the hypothesis that pensions and training are joint outcomes of employment contracts is strongly supported. The simple correlation between these two employment outcomes is high, and even controlling for wage income and other worker and firm characteristics, employees who received training are 7 percent more likely to be covered by a pension.

The prediction that pension coverage is more likely to be found where training is firm-specific was not confirmed. A ranking of training coefficient estimates by the degree of specificity was not consistent. We did find, on the other hand, evidence that workers with training were more likely to have defined-benefit coverage. This result is evidence that pension career incentives have a productivity function. It is difficult to explain this result without referencing defined-benefit tenure and retirement incentives.

NOTES

1. A good summary of these studies can be found in Gustman, Mitchell, and Steinmeier (1994). Some are identified in endnote 4 to Chapter 1 (p. 11).
2. Since the review of training studies in Brown (1990), notable recent efforts include Lynch (1992) and Bartel (1995).
3. In his model, training increases lifetime income, which generates a demand for pensions due to tax incentives. An implication of this demand-side model is that training increases the likelihood of both defined-contribution and defined-benefit plans.
4. Altonji and Spletzer (1991), using the NLS of 1972 High School Graduates, reported 28 percent receiving formal company training, 20 percent informal OJT, and 20 percent attending outside programs. Brown's (1990) survey found a range of company-provided training between 5 and 20 percent.
5. The pension coverage equation is identified because several variables that affect potential wage income can be excluded from the model of pension choice. The regressors in the structural wage equation included TRAINING, EDUCATION, MARRIED-SPOUSE PRESENT, AGE, AGE SQUARED, FEMALE, FIRM SIZE, UNION, TENURE, TENURE SQUARED, RACE, and INDUSTRY. Race

and several of the industry dummy variables have a significant effect on wage income but not on the likelihood of pension coverage. Reduced-form probit estimates of pension coverage and annual wage income are available from the authors.

6.   Some training that is reported as "occupation-specific," of course, could be transferable to other firms employing workers in the same occupation. Our test is based upon the idea that this category is more likely to include firm-specific training.

7   Note that the categories are not exclusive—a large number of observations reported training under more than one category.

7 Estimates of Pension Coverage and Productivity Differentials

The fundamental issue raised in this monograph is whether pension coverage can raise workforce productivity. Unfortunately, there is almost no direct evidence on whether firms that sponsor pensions realize productivity gains. This chapter is a step towards closing this gap in the empirical literature. The framework for our investigation is a production function that includes the firm's pension status as an additional argument. Estimates of the parameters associated with pension status allow us to determine if pension coverage is associated with higher labor productivity.

Because restrictions on quit and retirement decisions are costly to workers, theory predicts that these incentives must establish productivity gains at least sufficient to fund a compensating wage premium. If not, employers would sponsor incentive-neutral pension plans. If we do not find a productivity advantage for firms that sponsor defined-benefit plans, we can reject the supply-side hypothesis in favor of alternative theories of pensions, in which pension career incentives are costly side-effects.

Our empirical analysis was carried out on a sample of manufacturing firms drawn from the annual Compustat Industrial File that were observed over the period 1981–92. Compustat is the only dataset that combines information on output, inputs, and pension provision for individual firms. In addition, the fact that the sample is a panel—i.e., cross section/time series—allowed us to control for fixed unobserved firm characteristics that may be correlated with the decision to offer a pension plan.

Although the empirical study conducted in this chapter represents an advance over previous work, the results should be interpreted with the following qualifications in mind. First, one shortcoming of the Compustat data is that only firms that offer defined-benefit plans can be identified. Distinctions between firms that sponsor defined-contribution plans and those that do not provide a pension are not possible. Given that our sample is made up of large manufacturing firms, however, virtually all of those without defined-benefit plans will sponsor defined-contribution plans. Thus, the productivity differentials we estimate are between firms offering defined-benefit pensions and those offering defined-contribution coverage. Any estimated productivity differences should reflect defined-benefit tenure and retirement incentives.

Second, the decision to offer a pension plan clearly is not "exogenous." If the supply-side view of pensions is correct, firms that offer coverage will be those with expectations of productivity gains. Panel data will help to the extent that certain fixed firm characteristics can account for the decision to offer a pension. The pension-offer decision, however, may be too complicated to be captured simply through panel data estimation techniques. If this is so, a finding that firms with defined-benefit plans have higher labor productivity does not imply that *all* firms would benefit from pension incentives. Unfortunately, Compustat does not provide enough information to formally model a firm's pension sponsorship.

Keep in mind that our primary goal is simply to test whether or not firms that choose defined-benefit coverage are more productive. The productivity theory does not imply that all firms will experience productivity gains. Thus a positive pension coefficient, even if it is a biased estimate of the gain from sponsoring a defined-benefit plan for all firms, can still support the productivity theory.

A related problem is that the data do not allow tests of the channels through which gains may be realized. As we indicated in the first chapter, the ideal model would specify empirical connections from pension coverage to labor market outcomes; for example, to increased training, and then from the latter to improved productivity. The Compustat file does not, however, have information on turnover, training, effort, employee education levels, or other wage and human resource policies which may affect productivity. Our results will indicate whether labor productivity is greater in firms that sponsor defined-benefit coverage, but they cannot provide evidence on the source of these gains.

EMPIRICAL FRAMEWORK

Empirical Model

The productivity theory of pensions predicts that defined-benefit incentives for long tenure and early retirement will raise labor productivity. Whether and how the provision of defined-benefit pensions would affect capital use efficiency is not as clear. One possible channel might be complementarities between training and capital. In other words, investments in human capital may raise the productivity of capital equipment.[1]

The proposition that defined-benefit pension plans increase productivity can be tested by estimating a production function that includes the firm's pension status as an argument. The general form for such a model may be expressed as

Eq. 7.1 $\qquad Y_{it} = f(x_{it}, P_{it}, \tau)\exp(\varepsilon_{it}),$

where Y_{it} is firm i's ($i = 1, \ldots, N$) output in period t ($t = 1, \ldots, T$); x_{it} ($= x_{it1}, \ldots, x_{itJ}$) is a vector of inputs; P_{it} is a dummy variable equal to 1 if the firm offers a pension plan and 0 otherwise; τ is a trend capturing technical change (shifts in the production function over time), and ε_{it} is a random disturbance term. We also consider a general index for technical change that substitutes time dummy variables for the trend. The time dummies impose very little structure on the production function shifts, which may be beneficial when examining the temporal pattern of productivity differences.[2]

Estimation of the model depends upon a stochastic specification of the error term and an assumption about the functional form of the production function. The panel nature of our sample leads us to specify the disturbance in Eq. 7.1 as

Eq. 7.2 $\qquad \varepsilon_{it} = \alpha_i + v_{it},$

where α_i represents unobserved firm-specific characteristics that may be correlated with pension status or inputs and v_{it} represents the usual statistical noise.

The simplest assumption for the production function would be that technology is Cobb-Douglas, which leads to the following empirical model:

Eq. 7.3 $\ln y_{it} = \gamma_0 + \sum_{j=1}^{J} \gamma_j \ln x_{itj} + \gamma_t \tau + \gamma_P P_{it} + \varepsilon_{it}$.

In this case, the productivity differential between firms that do and do not offer a pension is a pure intercept shift and is measured by the estimated coefficient of P_{it}.

A drawback to the Cobb-Douglas model is that it cannot be used to test whether pension provision affects productivity differently through the capital or labor input. An alternative is to specify a flexible functional form for the production function. The translog functional form allows the pension variable to be interacted with the inputs and the time trend. The translog version of Eq. 7.1 can be written as

Eq. 7.4 $\ln y_{it} = \gamma_0 + \sum_{j=1}^{J} \gamma_j \ln x_{itj} + \gamma_t \tau + \gamma_P P_{it}$

$$+ \frac{1}{2} \sum_{j=1}^{J} \sum_{k=1}^{J} \gamma_{jk} \ln x_{itj} \ln x_{itk} + \frac{1}{2} \gamma_{tt} \tau^2$$

$$+ \sum_{j=1}^{J} \gamma_{jt} \ln x_{itj} \tau + \sum_{j=1}^{J} \gamma_{jp} \ln x_{itj} P_{it} + \varepsilon_{it} ,$$

where $\gamma_{jk} = \gamma_{kj}$.

Estimation

How Eq. 7.3 or 7.4 is to be estimated depends on how we treat the firm-specific component of the disturbance. The supply-side theory of pensions implies that pension status is likely correlated with the α_i; that is, firms that sponsor defined-benefit plans will be those most likely to translate the incentives into productivity gains. The main advantage of panel data is that the parameters of the production function can be estimated consistently, even in the presence of such correlation.

The most straightforward method for dealing with such correlation is to assume the α_i are *fixed* in the sample and estimate the production function—as specified in Eq. 7.1 or 7.4—conditioning on the effects. This can be accomplished by applying ordinary least squares (OLS) to model variables that have been transformed into deviations from firm means. This is the so-called "within" transformation, because it involves only the within-firm variation in the data. Hence, fixed-effects estimation requires that there be some time variation in the data. This implies that the effect of pensions on productivity will be estimated through firms' changes in pension status.

If the effects are uncorrelated with the explanatory variables, more statistically efficient estimates can be obtained by treating the α_i as a set of independent *random* variables. The random-effects version of the model is estimated by generalized least squares (GLS), which can also be computed by applying OLS to a simple data transformation. In this case, each variable is differenced using a factor that weights the contribution of within- and between-firm variation.[3] Thus, random-effects estimation does not depend on status changers to identify the coefficients of variables involving pension status. Nevertheless, the GLS estimates will be inconsistent if the regressors are correlated with any of the right-hand-side variables. Fortunately, this assumption can be can be tested by contrasting the fixed and random-effects estimates.[4]

EMPIRICAL EVIDENCE

Data

Our primary data source is the Compustat Annual Industrial file, which provides financial and market information for over 2,400 individual firms from 1973 to 1992. Compustat is the only dataset we are aware of that combines information on output, inputs, and pension provision for individual firms.[5] While the Compustat production data is available for the full 20 years, the pension data has been recorded only since 1981. Hence our sample period is 1981–92, so that $T = 12$.

From Compustat we obtain the following empirical measures of each firm's output (y_{it}) and inputs (x_{it}). Output is defined as net sales; the inputs, which are capital (K_{it}) and labor (L_{it}), are defined as the property, plant, and equipment and the number of employees, respectively. Compustat reports both gross and net property, plant, and equipment (the latter accounting for depreciation); we estimate our models alternating between the two measures. Summary statistics for the measures of output and inputs used in our empirical models are provided in Table 7.1.

Whether or not a firm offers a defined-benefit pension is not directly observable in the Compustat file, but data on plan assets are available. Depending on the Federal Accounting Standards Board (FASB) rule in force, one or two pension asset variables are recorded. Until 1985, firms simply reported net pension assets; from 1985 on, however, a distinction is made between over- and underfunded plan assets. A positive value for any one of these variables is indicative that a defined-benefit plan is provided.[6] Thus, we set P_{it} to 1 in any period for which a firm has positive pension assets and 0 otherwise. After elimi-

Table 7.1 Means of Variables, by Year[a]

Year	y ($, millions)	Gross K ($, millions)	Net K ($, millions)	L (thousands)
1981	1129.17	615.127	351.625	13.963
1982	1097.11	662.462	374.607	13.004
1983	1169.65	695.672	384.711	13.380
1984	1317.02	738.773	407.047	14.158
1985	1437.62	829.977	456.301	14.242
1986	1547.35	912.118	483.960	14.309
1987	1746.67	1016.66	520.242	14.378
1988	1950.34	1087.51	556.071	15.194
1989	2023.58	1148.37	592.188	15.448
1990	2226.13	1290.92	659.153	15.341
1991	2256.84	1390.27	694.825	14.832
1992	2339.53	1470.95	699.366	14.222

[a]y is net sales (gross sales reduced by cash and trade discounts, and returned sales and allowances for which credit is given); gross K is the cost of tangible fixed property (plant and equipment) used to produce revenue; net K is gross K less accumulated depreciation; and L is the number of employees. $N = 361$.

nating those firms with missing observations for output, capital, and labor, we are left with a balanced panel of 1130 firms.

One strategy would be to estimate our empirical model using all 1130 firms. However, proceeding as if a single production process governs output generation is questionable, because these firms represent every major industry category. An alternative strategy would be to estimate the model separately for each one-digit industry. This is problematic due to the limited number of firms and the small variation in P_{it} in some industry groups. As a compromise, we concentrate our attention on manufacturing (the largest one-digit industry category), resulting in a 12-year panel of 396 firms.

Given certain vagaries in the reporting of pension asset quantities, due in large part to the FASB rule changes, it is possible that some firms are misrepresented as terminating their defined-benefit plan during the sample period. This type of measurement error is particularly troublesome in fixed-effects regressions, so we corroborated the pension terminations, as revealed by changes in P_{it}, by referencing the Pension Benefit Guaranty Corporation's (PBGC) notification tape.[7]

Based on the notification tape, we could not verify plan cancellation for 36 firms. Removing these firms from the sample leaves us with a cross-section (N) of 361 firms, 40 of which changed pension status from 1981 to 1992. The latter group does not include firms that canceled defined-benefit plans only to establish new ones in the same or next year. In any case, coverage rates for these manufacturing firms remained relatively high over the period, ranging from 70 to 74 percent. Of the 40 changers, 18 dropped plans and 22 added plans.[8] Consistent with Mittelstaedt and Regier (1993), firms that dropped coverage had higher funding ratios, lower returns on assets, and smaller cash flows than firms that added plans. There was a great deal of similarity across these characteristics between firms that added plans and those that maintained coverage throughout the period, while firms that never offered a pension had lower returns on assets and smaller cash flows than either of the former.[9]

Estimation Results

In the simplest Cobb-Douglas model (Eq. 7.3), the pension effect is a pure intercept shift. In the translog model (Eq. 7.4), input elasticities and technical change vary with pension status. The latter is an important advantage. Theory predicts that productivity gains should be accomplished primarily through the labor input. Results that indicated similar productivity effects for labor and capital would be difficult to attribute to pension incentives.

We estimate each model under both fixed and random-effects assumptions, alternating between the gross and net capital measures, as well as trend and general index (time dummy) specifications of technical change. In each case, we test whether the explanatory variables are uncorrelated with the firm effects. A rejection of the null hypothesis would support basing inference on the fixed-effects estimates, since they are consistent under the alternative.

As a contrast to results obtained from panel data estimation procedures, we also report conventional OLS estimates. Since OLS ignores firm-specific unobservables entirely, like GLS, it will yield consistent estimates of the production function parameters only if the explanatory variables are uncorrelated with the firm effects. However, OLS weights the within- and between-firm variation in the data equally, whereas the panel data estimators give greater weight to the former. Thus, OLS is least dependent on pension status changes in the estimation of the pension coefficients.[10] Putting aside the issue of consistency, the OLS results will provide some indication of the sensitivity of the estimated pension effect to treatment of pension status changers.

We now summarize the evidence from our sample on the relationship between pension sponsorship and productivity. Table 7.2 reports the estimated pension coefficient from the Cobb-Douglas models. The fixed-effects estimates, which control for unobserved firm characteristics, indicate that pension status is a highly significant shifter of the production function. The coefficient estimates range from 0.056 to 0.072, depending on how capital is measured and technical change is specified. These estimates imply that the output of defined benefit firms is, on average, 6 to 7.6 percent higher than that of firms not offering a pension.

Both the GLS and OLS results, which do not condition on firm-specific unobservables, uniformly indicate a smaller pension effect. While the random-effects pension coefficient estimates remain positive and statistically significant, the OLS estimates suggest firms with pensions are less productive. However, when the net measure of capital is

Table 7.2 Cobb-Douglas Productivity Differentials

	OLS	Random effects	Fixed effects
Trend model			
Gross K measure	−0.0471	0.0422	0.0610
	(−3.7281)[a]	(2.5205)	(3.1244)
Net K measure	−0.0239	0.0668	0.0724
	(−1.8302)	(3.7500)	(3.6631)
General index model			
Gross K measure	−0.0475	0.0409	0.0560
	(−3.7651)	(2.3455)	(2.8915)
Net K measure	−0.0243	0.0640	0.0679
	(−1.8569)	(3.6128)	(3.4609)

[a]Numbers in parentheses are asymptotic t-statistics.

employed, the estimated OLS pension coefficient is not significant at the usual 5 percent level.

In moving from the fixed-effects to the GLS and then to the OLS estimator, progressively less (more) weight is given to the within-firm (between-firm) variation in the data. Thus, it appears as we rely less on pension status changers to identify the pension coefficients, we obtain smaller estimates of productivity differences. At the same time, not using within-firm information exclusively may lead to inconsistency, as described above. In fact, specification tests reject the hypothesis that the explanatory variables are uncorrelated with the effects.

While the evidence on an overall productivity-enhancing effect of pensions is somewhat mixed, the results on the connection between pensions and the productivity of labor are not. Table 7.3 reports the estimated coefficient of the labor-pension status interaction, $\hat{\gamma}_{LP}$, as obtained from the translog production function.[11] Regardless of the estimation procedure, technical change specification, or capital measure, pension status is shown to have a positive and statistically significant impact on the labor elasticity. Thus, whether we control for unobserved firm differences (fixed-effects) or not (GLS and OLS), the qualitative result remains, with the size of the estimated effect being approximately 7 to 16 percent.

Table 7.3 Effect of Pension Sponsorship on Labor Elasticity

	OLS	Random effects	Fixed effects
Trend model			
Gross K measure	0.1570	0.0889	0.0799
	(6.5204)[a]	(3.7596)	(3.2236)
Net K measure	0.0933	0.1153	0.1217
	(3.9527)	(4.9981)	(5.0263)
General index model			
Gross K measure	0.1529	0.0794	0.0704
	(6.3185)	(3.3481)	(2.8345)
Net K measure	0.0894	0.1078	0.1146
	(3.7680)	(4.6650)	(4.7290)

[a]Numbers in parentheses are asymptotic t-statistics.

Interestingly, the largest coefficient estimates are generated by OLS (using the gross capital measure). On the face of it, this appears difficult to reconcile with the OLS Cobb-Douglas results in Table 7.2. However, as in the Cobb-Douglas model, OLS estimation of the translog produces a negative estimate of the intercept shift term, $\hat{\gamma}_P$. In this case, $\hat{\gamma}_P$ partially offsets the productivity-enhancing effect of pension provision on labor.

In sum, the translog estimates provide some evidence that the presence of a defined-benefit pension plan enhances productivity overall and strongly suggest that pensions raise labor productivity. What remains is to clarify the magnitude and temporal pattern of the productivity differential between firms that do and do not offer pensions.

Tables 7.4 and 7.5 list the estimated productivity differentials for each period in the sample, as implied by the translog models, using the results from the trend and general index specifications, respectively.[12] The estimated productivity differentials based on the fixed-effects estimates are listed in the last column. Consistent with the fixed-effects Cobb-Douglas results, these estimated differentials are positive in every case except one. However, the average productivity gains suggested by the translog models are smaller. When technical change is modeled in terms of a trend, the mean differential is 4.4 (5.8) percent when the gross (net) measure of capital is used. Utilizing a general

Table 7.4 Translog Productivity Differentials Trend Model

Year	OLS	Random effects	Fixed effects
Gross capital measure			
1981	−0.0177	0.0538	0.0700
1982	−0.0352	0.0426	0.0581
1983	−0.0350	0.0414	0.0551
1984	−0.0307	0.0426	0.0542
1985	−0.0390	0.0366	0.0469
1986	−0.0442	0.0323	0.0412
1987	−0.0448	0.0308	0.0378
1988	−0.0390	0.0329	0.0379
1989	−0.0392	0.0316	0.0350
1990	−0.0415	0.0292	0.0310
1991	−0.0439	0.0269	0.0272
1992	−0.0462	0.0246	0.0234
Net capital measure			
1981	0.0361	0.1208	0.1314
1982	0.0187	0.0991	0.1065
1983	0.0125	0.0914	0.0963
1984	0.0076	0.0854	0.0879
1985	−0.0047	0.0703	0.0700
1986	−0.0136	0.0593	0.0563
1987	−0.0195	0.0518	0.0462
1988	−0.0227	0.0475	0.0396
1989	−0.0300	0.0380	0.0275
1990	−0.0362	0.0295	0.0164
1991	−0.0410	0.0220	0.0063
1992	−0.0471	0.0134	−0.0050

Table 7.5 Translog Productivity Differentials General Index Model

Year	OLS	Random effects	Fixed effects
Gross capital measure			
1981	0.0049	0.0740	0.0908
1982	0.0019	0.0620	0.0734
1983	−0.0423	0.0156	0.0243
1984	−0.0364	0.0239	0.0316
1985	−0.0593	0.0180	0.0267
1986	−0.0691	0.0159	0.0244
1987	−0.1106	−0.0166	−0.0105
1988	−0.0543	0.0276	0.0300
1989	−0.0321	0.0487	0.0482
1990	0.0006	0.0543	0.0520
1991	−0.0189	0.0321	0.0278
1992	−0.0445	0.0085	0.0041
Net capital measure			
1981	0.0604	0.1413	0.1523
1982	0.0552	0.1205	0.1227
1983	0.0110	0.0690	0.0672
1984	0.0113	0.0707	0.0679
1985	−0.0227	0.0544	0.0532
1986	−0.0495	0.0354	0.0351
1987	−0.1007	−0.0053	−0.0087
1988	−0.0443	0.0387	0.0276
1989	−0.0229	0.0549	0.0400
1990	0.0103	0.0560	0.0375
1991	−0.0122	0.0284	0.0070
1992	−0.0392	0.0025	−0.0195

index of technical change causes the mean differential to fall to 3.6 (4.9) percent.

In the first two columns of Tables 7.4 and 7.5, the implied differentials from the OLS and random-effects regressions are listed. The mean random-effects-based differentials are similar in magnitude to the those derived from the fixed-effects estimates. The mean differential is 3.6 (6.3) percent using a trend specification and gross capital and 3.1 (5.7) percent using a general index. The OLS-based differentials are negative for all periods except the early years of the sample period. At the mean, the productivity differentials obtained from OLS range from −3.9 to −1.1 percent. Recall that even the OLS results, however, find a positive effect on labor productivity.

Finally, there is one sense in which all three sets of estimates agree: that the temporal pattern of the productivity differential is one of steady decline. This is generally true even under the time-dummy specification, which does not impose any structure on the temporal pattern of the differential. The decline in the differential parallels the fall in defined-benefit coverage during the 1980s.

SUMMARY

This chapter has presented new empirical evidence on the relationship between pensions and productivity. Our empirical framework has been a production function that includes the firm's pension status as an argument. Using a 12-year panel of Compustat manufacturing firms, we estimated the production function under different assumptions about functional form, the capital measure, and the role of unobserved firm characteristics.

Our main empirical finding is that labor appears to be more productive in firms with defined-benefit pensions, which is consistent with the productivity theory of pensions. This result does not depend on the estimation technique or the measure of capital employed. The evidence on the effect of pensions on overall productivity is more mixed. Fixed-effects estimation leads to average productivity differentials of 5 to 8 percent, while estimation procedures that do not control for firm unobservables indicate smaller (and in some cases, negative) productivity differences.

Of course, other stories can be invoked to explain these findings. An alternative theory is that defined-benefit coverage may proxy for an entire package of human resource policies (sometimes called "best practice") that promotes productivity. "Progressive" firms provide more generous benefit packages, including pensions, and have more enlightened and effective workplace policies, according to this view. High-compensation firms also may attract higher-quality workers and have more selective hiring policies. A variant of this idea is that pension coverage represents an "efficiency wage," and it is this premium pay that creates incentives for long tenure or greater effort.

Testing these competing theories would require detailed, firm-level data on workforce characteristics, compensation and benefits, and other human resource policies. One might argue, however, that differences in human resource policies between the large firms in our sample will be modest. And, if these policies do not change with pension coverage, the fixed-effects estimation should provide a consistent estimate of the overall productivity differential.

Finally, regardless of how the estimation is carried out, the data reveal a fairly sharp decline in the productivity differentials over the sample period. For example, the fixed-effects estimates of the productivity differential fall from 15 percent in 1981 to essentially zero in 1992. One implication of this result is that the productivity differences between firms that sponsor defined-benefit versus defined-contribution plans has narrowed significantly. It is natural to speculate whether the diminishing differential is in some way related to the decline in defined-benefit coverage that occurred over the same period. An intriguing possibility is the implication that the productivity costs of switching to a defined-contribution plan generally declined over the during the 1980s.

NOTES

1. A similar strategy was used by Ichniowski, Shaw, and Prennushi (1977) to assess the effects of various human resource management practices, such as incentive pay and teamwork.

2. The general index of technical change allows for greater temporal flexibility in the production function but at the cost of greatly increasing the number of parameters. See Baltagi and Griffin (1988).

3. For any variable, say z_{it}, this data transformation creates

$$z_{it}^* = \tilde{z}_{it} + \theta \bar{z}_i = z_{it} - (1 - \theta) z_i,$$

where

the deviations from firm means, $\tilde{z}_i = z_{it} - \bar{z}_i$,

the firm means $\bar{z}_i = T^{-1} \Sigma_t z_{it}$,

$\theta = [\sigma_v^2 / (\sigma_v^2 + T\sigma_\omega^2)]^{1/2}$,

σ_α^2 is the variance of α_i, and

σ_v^2 is the variance of v_{it}.

The relationship between the fixed-effects and GLS estimators is easily seen in light of this data transformation, since the former can be obtained by setting θ to 0.

4. The Wu-Hausman test-statistic for null hypothesis of no correlation between the regressors and the effects is $\hat{q}' [\text{cov}(\hat{q})]^{-1} \hat{q}$, where $\hat{q}$ is the difference between the fixed-effects and random-effects coefficient vectors and $\text{cov}(\hat{q})$ is the covariance matrix of $\hat{q}$.

5. These data have been used in a similar fashion by Kruse (1991) and Kumbhakar and Dunbar (1993) to examine the productivity effects of ESOPs.

6. We are grateful to Fred Mittelstaedt for his help in interpreting the Compustat pension data.

7. We thank Dick Ippolito of the PBGC for providing us with a copy of the tape.

8. The essentially equal representation among the plan terminators and new sponsors may be surprising. It is possible, however, that some of the firms not confirmed as plan terminators through the PBGC termination tape actually did drop coverage. In any case, including these firms in our empirical analysis does not alter the results in any meaningful way.

9. We computed the funding ratio as net pension assets divided by the sum of vested and nonvested benefits, return on assets as the ratio of dividends to assets, and cash flow as the ratio of funds from operations to assets.

10. Note that OLS can be understood in terms of the random-effects data transformation with θ set to 1, so that $z_{it}^* = z_{it} = \tilde{z}_{it} + \bar{z}_i$. See note 3 above.

11. Note that, in every instance, the restrictions imposed by the Cobb-Douglas functional form are not supported by the data.

12. The expression for the productivity differential is

$$E(\ln y \mid P = 1) - E(\ln y \mid P = 0) = \gamma_P + \gamma_{KP} \ln K_{it} + \gamma_{LP} \ln L_{it} + \gamma_{tP} \tau,$$

where, in the general index model, D_t is substituted for τ.

8 Summary and Conclusions

Research on the economics of pensions has yielded several reasons why some firms sponsor pensions and others do not. One set of theories can be labeled broadly as demand-side: employees value pension benefits more than current wages. Considerable evidence supports the tax theory of pensions. But pensions became popular before there was a federal income tax. In addition, the pension plan preferred by most firms has features that cannot be explained by favorable tax rules. Defined-benefit plans with delayed vesting dominated the pension market for decades.

A supply-side conjecture has been that pensions reward employee behavior that raises productivity. Since pensions are voluntary, it is natural for economists to seek an explanation of pension incentives that is grounded in efficiency. This perspective has been encouraged by the popularity of internal labor market models, in which gains result from long-term employment.

This manuscript has attempted a careful assessment of the productivity perspective on pensions. We have explored this theory of pensions in three parts. First, the institutional features of pensions were reviewed and we demonstrated how pensions penalize early separation and late retirement. Second, we compared pension incentives to severance penalties and retirement bonuses predicted by internal labor market models. Third, we reviewed evidence on pensions and reported some new empirical results. In this final chapter we summarize what is known about pensions and productivity and suggest directions for future research.

Our most basic and least controversial result is that defined-benefit plans reward long tenure and penalize late retirement. This is hardly original. However, we were surprised that career incentives of defined-benefit plans have received little attention in the human resource literature. Also, there is disagreement over whether pension incentives are valuable or whether nonportable pensions, in addition to lowering benefits, reduce productive efficiency by locking workers into jobs. The latter perspective suggests that defined-benefit separation penalties are unintended or unavoidable. Our review suggested, however, that defined-benefit incentives could be reduced or eliminated. If the costs of nonportability were not offset by gains elsewhere, employers would be expected to implement incentive-neutral plans. At the least, employers easily could have adopted early vesting before required to do so by regulations.

We found that pension incentives generally are consistent with the firm-specific training model. The pension quit penalty may serve as a severance tax, which discourages workers from moving to jobs where their productivity would be lower and, in effect, insures the firm's training investments. A problem for this theory, however, is that the quit penalty is low for recent hires and may be insufficient to prevent quits of workers whose productivity peaks early. The separation penalty also will not, by itself, deter shirking by recent hires. Both of these models predict severance payments to encourage early retirement, as indeed would any long-term employment model in which wages were inflexible downward. There seems to be general agreement among economists and practitioners that pension retirement incentives are valuable.

Unfortunately, there is little clear-cut evidence with which to evaluate the importance of pension incentives or to test the productivity perspective against other pension theories. Direct tests of whether workers or firms are more productive when pensions are part of the compensation package are virtually nonexistent. This shortcoming, which extends to wage policies generally, largely reflects data limitations.

The ideal empirical test would be based on a structural model of pension coverage, worker behavior, and a production function which translated improved employee outcomes to output gains. This model would reveal *how* pension coverage influenced productivity by specifying mechanisms (such as reduced employee turnover or shirking, increased training investments, induced retirement, or attracting workers who are inherently more productive) that could be tested directly. It also would recognize that pension coverage is endogenous, requiring that we estimate pension choices as a function of potential output gains, as well as of other firm and employee characteristics suggested by demand-side theories of pension coverage. Such a model would be capable of comparing the relative importance of the productivity function with other pension theories.

The data required to estimate this fully specified model are ambitious. Gustman and Mitchell (1992) list information on firms' output, capital inputs, other human resource policies, and financial characteristics, at a minimum. A rich set of employee characteristics also is necessary, not only because individuals differ in productivity but also because factors such as income and marital status influence the demand for pension coverage. Since many important firm and employee characteristics are unobservable, a longitudinal data file would be necessary.

No data set came close to allowing us to estimate a structural empirical model. We did report, however, results from a production function model, which compared labor productivity in firms that sponsored defined-benefit pensions with those that did not. Cross-section and panel estimates suggested that defined-benefit plans are associated with a more efficient workforce.

We believe that these results are interesting and advance the empirical literature on pensions, but they clearly fall short of the ideally specified model. We had no ability to assess the channels through which productivity gains were realized, and the data did not allow modeling pension plan choice or, in the case of the longitudinal estimates, the decision to change plans. Another problem was that, in this sample, firms that did not sponsor defined-benefit plans probably had defined-contribution pensions. We have raised the possibility that the former may promote productivity gains, but we were unable to test for differences between firms that sponsor a defined-contribution plan and those that have no pension.

For the near future, empirical evidence on pensions is likely to be indirect or based on reduced-form estimates. We believe that the bulk of this evidence supports the conclusion that, for whatever reason, workers in jobs with pensions are more productive than uncovered workers. In addition to the estimates presented in Chapter 7, several studies find that favorable labor market outcomes are associated with pensions. There is clear evidence that pension-covered workers receive significantly higher wages, and they are less likely to quit or to be laid off.

But the channels which generate these outcomes remain largely shrouded in a "black box." We investigated one of these channels, reporting evidence of a robust relationship between pensions and employee training. We also found that training raised the probability of defined-benefit coverage, a result consistent with the theory that employers use pensions to discourage quits of valued workers. On the other hand, we also found that trained workers were more likely to have a defined-contribution pension than no coverage. This result may reflect that defined-contribution pensions attract "low discounters," who are less likely to quit, or that pension benefits are part of an overall compensation premium designed to discourage quits. The data do not allow us to distinguish between these explanations.

PENSION POLICY AND RECOMMENDATIONS FOR FUTURE RESEARCH

We do not claim that the suggestive evidence we have reviewed and presented supports hard policy recommendations. Research on the value of specific pension incentive mechanisms is needed and should be at the top of the agenda for research on pensions and productivity. Investigating the "black box" would raise our understanding of the economics of pensions and inform analysis of the effects of pension policy.

Congress has enacted or considered a number of policies which would dilute or eliminate pension incentives. These include shortening vesting periods, eliminating penalties for late retirement, making pension service credit under defined-benefit plans transferable, and a series of changes to the tax and regulatory codes which have raised the cost of administering plans, especially those providing defined benefits. The principal policy implication of the productivity perspective on pensions is that these policies may have an output cost. It is not possible, however, to predict with any precision the size of the productivity costs of reduced defined-benefit incentives.

This is especially true of policies which apparently have encouraged the substitution of defined-contribution coverage. The latter do not have tenure or retirement incentives but may be more efficient at attracting more productive employees. 401(k) plans, which have been encouraged by regulatory policy, seem to be particularly well-suited for this purpose. If this channel is more important, the productivity costs of moving to defined-contribution coverage may be minimal; we simply do not have enough information about the importance of pension incentives to make a judgement.

Some policy makers have advocated reduction or elimination of favorable tax treatment of private-sector pension compensation in general. The revenue loss from this "tax expenditure" is over $25 billion, one of the largest in the federal income tax code, and is a tempting target for revenue enhancement. Defenders of the pension tax subsidy have emphasized the importance of pensions in providing retirement income security, but there also may be some productivity costs from policies that reduce the attractiveness of defined-benefit and defined-contribution coverage.

At the same time, the productivity hypothesis suggests that coverage is not solely a function of a favorable tax code. Many firms would continue to sponsor pensions, even if the tax subsidy were eliminated, just as pension sponsorship grew early in the century before the federal income tax was enacted.

The current lack of understanding of the channels through which pensions may encourage productivity makes it difficult to predict the future of defined-benefit plans. Primary defined-benefit coverage has declined steadily over the past two decades. Evidence suggests that this reflects structural changes in the labor market and policies that have raised the relative cost and lowered tax advantages of defined-benefit coverage. Defined-contribution growth has occurred primarily in sectors where productivity gains from defined-benefit incentives were arguably smaller. We conclude that the trend to primary defined-contribution coverage is not *prima facie* evidence of a declining importance for productivity incentives.

Yet we do not have direct evidence that incentives are a major factor in continued sponsorship of defined-benefit plans by larger firms. Are tenure and retirement incentives, along with demand-side benefits such as insurance and risk-shifting, large enough to maintain an important market share for defined-benefit pensions? The future of defined-benefit plans is made more uncertain by the apparent substitution of 401(k) plans, which may have productivity advantages of their own, by firms that would otherwise been likely to sponsor the traditional defined-benefit plans. 401(k) plans have opened avenues for further growth of primary defined-contribution coverage.

Clearly, significant progress in testing theories of pensions requires a rich data set along the lines suggested by Gustman and Mitchell. However, it is questionable if even a major investment in new data would allow estimation of a fully specified structural model of pension coverage and its effects.   Firm- and individual-specific effects will be of critical importance in measuring productivity differences, as will other factors that affect the supply and demand for pension coverage. The problem is that these factors are difficult to measure even with detailed data on individuals and firms.   What is a good proxy for an internal rate of discount or the degree of risk preference? What job characteristics suggest the extent of potential gains from firm-specific training or early retirement? The inherent difficult of measuring these attributes makes it a challenge to create reliable instruments to identify the structural parameters of a pension model.

It is likely that better data for testing pension theories will come as a by-product of research on productivity effects of more general compensation policies. We have noted the lack of evidence on the incentive effects of merit pay, bonuses, wage-seniority profiles, gainsharing, and other human resource policies.   A data set capable of testing for these more direct incentives must meet the requirements described above. While research on these issues is a high priority, we would urge investigators to include as much information as possible on pension policies when gathering data on employer compensation policies.

Short of exploiting the ideal data set, there may be opportunities for more powerful reduced-form or indirect tests of pension/productivity channels. Our test of the relationship between pensions and training was crude. More refined estimates would be possible with detailed firm-level data on pension rules and the type and level of training. Recall that the ideal quit penalty matches the value of the firm's investment, implying greater pension losses in jobs where the firm-specific investments are greater. Another testable prediction with better training data is that, since the pension loss typically peaks late in the career, defined-benefit coverage should be more likely in jobs where training is gradual and productivity peaks late in the career.

While it is widely accepted that pensions can encourage early withdrawal of older workers from the labor force, not much is known about the value of this incentive. Considerable evidence indicates that workers respond to retirement incentives, but there is almost no evidence on why some firms establish these incentives and others do not. Empirical evidence on whether retirement incentives reflect gains from early retirement would raise our understanding of defined-benefit plans. An example of such a test would be whether or not pension retirement incentives are more likely in jobs where human capital skills depreciate more rapidly.

Our impression is that research on whether pensions attract workers who are inherently more productive (low discounters) has the greatest potential. This conjecture is suggested by several pension studies that find favorable outcomes related to defined-contribution plans. Empirical labor studies have shown that unobservable, individual-specific attributes have major effects on wages and other outcomes. Finally, research from the field of psychology has suggested that one of the unobservable differences that may be associated with important differences in success is an individual's willingness to delay gratification. If the latter is true, potential gains from attracting such patient workers probably are much larger than those created by tenure and retirement incentives. But there is no concrete evidence that pension selectivity incentives are important.

Another avenue to increasing our understanding of pensions and productivity, short of a structural model, is the case study. While not widely used by economists, case studies are relatively common in the management literature, so we were surprised to find no analyses of organizations that sponsored pension plans. Case studies are by definition narrow in scope and the results are difficult to generalize, but given our ignorance about the effects of specific pension incentives and the size of resulting productivity gains (if any), this method may yield useful information.

There should be plenty of opportunities to observe effects of changes in pension incentives, since many firms recently have switched from defined-benefit to defined-contribution coverage. A case study could address such questions as: Why did the firm change coverage? Were productivity consequences considered? Have there been measurable effects on quit rates, retirement, and labor productivity? Has the sponsor adopted other incentives to encourage early retirement? Results from well-chosen case studies may direct some light on the "black box" and suggest the most promising approaches for future research on pensions and productivity.

REFERENCES

Akerlof, George A., and Lawrence F. Katz. 1989. "Workers' Trust Funds and the Logic of Wage Profiles." *Quarterly Journal of Economics* 106(August): 525–536.

Allen, Steven G., and Robert L. Clark. 1987. "Pensions and Firm Performance." In *Human Resources and The Performance of the Firm*, Morris Kleiner, et al., eds. Madison, Wisconsin: Industrial Relations Research Association, pp. 195–242.

Allen, Steven G., Robert L. Clark, and Ann A. McDermed. 1992. "Post-Retirement Benefit Increases in the 1980s." In *Trends in Pensions*, John Turner and Dan Beller, eds. Washington, D.C.: Government Printing Office, pp. 319–329.

———. 1993. "Pensions, Bonding, and Lifetime Jobs." *Journal of Human Resources* 28(Summer): 463–481.

Allen, Steven G., Robert L. Clark, and Daniel A. Sumner. 1986. "Post Retirement Adjustment of Pension Benefits." *Journal of Human Resources* 21(Winter): 118–137.

Alpert, William T. 1983. "Manufacturing Workers' Private Wage Supplements: A Simultaneous Equations Approach." *Applied Economics* 15(June): 363–378.

Altonji, Joseph, and James Spletzer. 1991. "Worker Characteristics, Job Characteristics, and the Receipt of On-the-Job Training." *Industrial and Labor Relations Review* 45(October): 58–79.

Arnott, Richard, Arthur J. Hosios, and Joseph Stiglitz. 1988. "Implicit Contracts, Labor Mobility, and Unemployment." *American Economic Review* 78(December): 1046–1066.

Asch, Beth J. 1990. "Do Incentives Matter? The Case of Navy Recruiters." *Industrial and Labor Relations Review* 4(February): S89–S106.

Atkins, Lawrence G. 1986. *Spend It Or Save It? Pension Lump-Sum Distributions and Tax Reform.* Washington, D.C.: Employee Benefit Research Institute.

Baltagi, Padi, and James Griffin. 1988. "A General Index of Technical Change." *Journal of Political Economy* 96(February): 20–41.

Bartel, Ann P. 1994. "Productivity Gains from the Implementation of Employee Training Programs." *Industrial Relations* 33(October): 411–425.

———. 1995. "Training, Wage Growth, and Job Performance: Evidence from a Company Database." *Journal of Labor Economics* 13(July): 401–425.

Becker, Gary. 1964. *Human Capital: A Theoretical and Empirical Analysis.* New York: Columbia University Press.

Becker, Gary, and George Stigler. 1974. "Law Enforcement, Malfeasance and Compensation of Officers." *Journal of Legal Studies* 3(1): 1–18.

Ben-Porath, Yoram. 1967. "The Production of Human Capital and the Life Cycle of Earnings." *Journal of Political Economy* 75(March): 352–365.

Beller, Daniel J., and Helen Lawrence. 1992. "Trends in Private Pension Plan Coverage." In *Trends in Pensions,* John Turner and Daniel Beller, eds. Washington, D.C.: Government Printing Office.

Bishop, John H. 1990. "Job Performance, Turnover, and Wage Growth." *Journal of Labor Economics* 8(July): 363–386.

Blinder, Alan S. 1982. "Private Pensions and Public Pensions: Theory and Fact." Working Paper No. 902. Cambridge, Massachusetts: National Bureau of Economic Research.

Blinder, Alan S., ed. 1990. *Paying for Productivity: A Look at the Evidence.* Washington, D.C.: The Brookings Institution.

Bodie, Zvi. 1990. "Pensions as Retirement Income Insurance." *Journal of Economic Literature* 37(March): 23–49.

Brennan, Lawrence T. 1984. "Updating the Traditional Corporation Retirement Plan, Part 1." *Compensation Review* 16(First Quarter): 11–25.

Brown, Charles. 1990. "Empirical Evidence on Private Training." In *Research in Labor Economics*, Volume 11, Lauri Bassi, ed. Greenwich, Connecticut: JAI Press.

Carmichael, H. Lorne. 1989. "Self–Enforcing Contracts, Shirking, and Life Cycle Incentives." *Journal of Economic Perspectives* 3(Fall): 972–990.

Choate, Pat, and J.K. Linger. 1986. *The Hi–Flex Society.* New York: Alfred A. Knopf.

Clark, Robert L., and Ann A. McDermed. 1990. *The Choice of Pension Plans in a Changing Regulatory Environment.* Washington, D.C.: American Enterprise Institute.

Cornwell, Christopher, Stuart Dorsey, and Nasser Mehrzad. 1991. "Opportunistic Behavior by Firms in Implicit Pension Contracts." *Journal of Human Resources* 26(Fall): 704–725.

Curme, Michael A., and William E. Even. 1995. "Pension Coverage and Borrowing Constraints." *Journal of Human Resources* 30(Fall): 701–712.

Doescher, Tabitha. 1994. "Are Pension Coverage Rates Declining?" In *Pension Coverage Issues for the '90s,* John Hinz, ed. Washington, D.C.: Government Printing Office.

Doescher, Tabitha, and Stuart Dorsey. 1992. "Pension Benefit Losses and Offsetting Compensation." Unpublished report, Pension and Welfare Benefits Administration, U.S. Department of Labor.

Dorsey, Stuart. 1982. "A Model and Empirical Estimates of Worker Pension Coverage in the U.S." *Southern Economic Journal* 49(October): 506–520.

———. 1987. "The Economic Function of Private Pensions: An Empirical Analysis." *Journal of Labor Economics* 5(October): S171–S89.

———. 1989. "A Test for a Wage-Pension Trade-off with Endogenous Pension Coverage." Baldwin City, Kansas: Baker University. Mimeographed.

———. 1995. "Pension Portability and Labor Market Efficiency: A Review of the Literature." *Industrial and Labor Relations Review* 48(January): 276–292.

Dorsey, Stuart, and David A. Macpherson. 1997. "Pensions and Training." *Industrial Relations* 36(January): 81–96.

Ehrenberg, Ronald G., and George T. Milkovich. 1987. "Compensation and Firm Performance." In *Human Resources and the Performance of the Firm*, Morris Kleiner et al., eds. Madison, Wisconsin: Industrial Relations Research Association, pp. 87–122.

Ehrenberg, Ronald G., and Robert S. Smith. 1997. *Modern Labor Economics*. Sixth Ed. Addison-Wesley.

EBRI. 1993. *Pension Evolution in a Changing Economy*. Washington, D.C.: Employee Benefits Research Institute.

———. 1997. *EBRI Databook on Employee Benefits*. Fourth Ed. Washington, D.C.: Employee Benefits Research Institute.

Even, William, and David Macpherson. 1990. "The Gender Gap in Pensions and Wages." *Review of Economics and Statistics* 72(May): 259–265.

———. 1994. "The Pension Coverage of Young and Mature Workers." In *Pension Coverage Issues for the '90s*, John Hinz, ed. Washington, D.C.: Government Printing Office.

———. 1996. "Employer Size and Labor Turnover: The Role of Pensions." *Industrial and Labor Relations Review* 49(July): 707–728.

Fields, Gary, and Olivia Mitchell. 1984. *Retirement, Pensions, and Social Security*. Cambridge, Massachusetts: MIT Press.

Flanagan, Robert. 1984. "Implicit Contracts, Explicit Contracts, and Wages." *American Economic Review* 74(May): 345–349.

Freeman, Richard B. 1985. "Unions, Pensions, and Union Pension Funds." In *Pensions, Labor, and Individual Choice,* David A. Wise, ed. Chicago: University of Chicago Press.

Goodfellow, Gordon P., and Sylvester Schieber. 1993. "Death and Taxes: Can We Fund for Retirement between Them?" In *The Future of Pensions in the United States*, Ray Schmitt, ed. Philadelphia: The Pension Research Council.

Grad, Susan. 1996. *Income of the Population 55 and Over, 1993.* U.S. Department of Health and Human Resources, Social Security Administration. Washington, D.C.: Government Printing Office.

Graebner, William. 1980. *A History of Retirement.* New Haven: Yale University Press.

Gratton, Brian. 1990. "A Triumph in Modern Philanthropy: Age Criteria in Labor Management at the Pennsylvania Railroad, 1875–1930." *Business History Review* 64(Winter): 630–656.

Gustman, Alan L., and Olivia S. Mitchell. 1992. "Pensions and the Labor Market: Behavior and Data Requirements." In *Pensions and the U.S. Economy: The Need for Good Data,* Zvi Bodie and Alicia Munnell, eds. Philadelphia: Pension Research Council, pp. 39–87.

Gustman, Alan L., Olivia S. Mitchell, and Thomas L. Steinmeier. 1994. "The Role of Pensions in the Labor Market: A Survey of the Literature." *Industrial and Labor Relations Review* 47(April): 417–438.

Gustman, Alan L., and Thomas L. Steinmeier. 1992. "The Stampede Towards Defined Contribution Pension Plans: Fact or Fiction?" *Industrial Relations* 31(Spring): 361–369.

———. 1995. *Pension Incentives and Job Mobility.* Kalamazoo, Michigan: W.E. Upjohn Institute for Employment Research.

Hall, Robert. 1980. "Employment Fluctuations and Wage Rigidity." *Brookings Papers on Economic Activity* (No. 1): 91–123.

Hall, Robert, and Edward P. Lazear. 1984. "The Excess Sensitivity of Layoffs and Quits to Demand." *Journal of Labor Economics* 2(April): 233–58.

Hannah, Leslie. 1986. *Inventing Retirement.* Mimeographed. New York City.

Hay/Huggins Company, Inc. 1990. *Pension Plan Expense Study for the Pension Benefit Guaranty Corporation.* Washington, D.C: Pension Benefit Guaranty Corporation.

Holmstrom, Bengt. 1983. "Equilibrium Long Term Contracts." *Quarterly Journal of Economics* 48(August): 23–54.

Holzer, Harry. 1990. "The Determinants of Employee Productivity and Earnings." *Industrial Relations* 29(Fall): 403–422.

Hutchens, Robert M. 1987. "A Test of Lazear's Theory of Delayed Payment Contracts." *Journal of Labor Economics* 5(October): S153–S170.

Ichniowski, Corey, Kathryn Shaw, and Giovanna Prennushi. 1997. "The Effects of Human Resource Management Practices on Productivity: A Study of Steel Finishing Lines." *American Economic Review* 87(June): 291–313.

Ippolito, Richard. 1985. "The Labor Contract and True Economic Pension Liabilities." *American Economic Review* 75(December): 1031–1043.

————. 1986. *Pensions, Economics and Public Policy.* Homewood, Illinois: Dow Jones-Irwin.

————. 1991a. "Encouraging Long-Term Tenure: Wage Tilt or Pensions?" *Industrial and Labor Relations Review* 44(April): 520–535.

————. 1991b. "The Productive Inefficiency of New Pension Tax Policy." *National Tax Journal* 64(September): 405–417.

————. 1994. "Pensions, Sorting and Indenture Premia." *Journal of Human Resources* 29(Summer): 795–812.

————. 1995. "Toward Explaining the Growth of Defined Contribution Plans." *Industrial Relations* 34(January): 1–20.

————. Forthcoming. *Pension Plans and Employee Performance.* Chicago: University of Chicago Press.

Ito, Takatoshi. 1988. "Labor Contracts with Voluntary Quits." *Journal of Labor Economics* 6(January): 100–131.

Johnson, Richard W. 1996. "The Impact of Human Capital Investments on Pension Benefits." *Journal of Labor Economics* 14(July): 520–554.

Jones, Derek C., Takao Kato, and Jeffrey Pliskin. 1997. "Profit Sharing and Gainsharing: A Review of Theory, Evidence and Effects." In *Handbook of Human Resources*, Part 1, D. Lewis, D. Mitchell, and M. Zaidi, eds. Greenwich, Connecticut: JAI Press, pp. 153–174.

Kahn, Charles. 1985. "Optimal Severance Pay with Incomplete Information." *Journal of Political Economy* 93(June): 435–456.

Kahn, Lawrence M., and Peter D. Sherer. 1990. "Contingent Pay and Managerial Performance." *Industrial and Labor Relations Review* 43(February): S107–S120.

Kennan, John. 1979. "Bonding and the Enforcement of Labor Contracts." *Economics Letters* 3(1979): 61–66.

Kolodrubetz, Walter W., and Donald M. Landay. 1973. "Coverage and Vesting of Full-Time Employees under Private Retirement Plans." *Social Security Bulletin* 36(November): 20–36.

Kotlikoff, Laurence J., and David A. Wise. 1987. "The Incentive Effects of Private Pension Plans." In *Issues in Pension Economics*, Zvi Bodie, John B. Shoven, and David A. Wise, eds. Chicago: University of Chicago Press, pp. 283–336.

Kruse, Douglas. 1991. "Profit Sharing in the 1980s: Disguised Wages or a Fundamentally Different Form of Compensation?" In *Structural Changes in U.S. Labor Markets*, Randall W. Eberts and Erica L. Groshen, eds. Armonk, New York: M. E. Sharpe, pp. 67–100.

————. 1992. "Profit Sharing and Productivity: Microeconomic Evidence from the United States." *The Economic Journal* 102(January): 22–36.

————. 1993. "Does Profit Sharing Affect Productivity?" Working Paper No. 4542. Cambridge, Massachusetts: National Bureau of Economic Research.

Kumbhakar, Subal C., and Amy E. Dunbar. 1993. "The Elusive ESOP-Productivity Link." *Journal of Public Economics* 52(2): 273–283.

Latimer, Murray W. 1932. *Industrial Pension Systems in the United States and Canada.* New York: Industrial Relations Counselors, Inc.

Lazear, Edward. 1979. "Why is There Mandatory Retirement?" *Journal of Political Economy* 87(December): 1261–1284.

————. 1983. "Pensions as Severance Pay." In *Financial Aspects of the United States Pension System*, Zvi Bodie and John Shoven, eds. Chicago: University of Chicago Press, pp. 163–188.

————. 1990. "Pensions and Deferred Benefits as Strategic Compensation." *Industrial Relations* 29(Spring): 263–280.

————. 1991. "Labor Economics and the Psychology of Organizations." *Journal of Economic Perspectives* 5(Spring): 89–110.

Lazear, Edward P., and Robert Moore. 1988. "Pensions and Mobility." In *Pensions in the U.S. Economy*, Zvi Bodie, et al., eds. Chicago: University of Chicago Press, pp. 163–188.

Long, James E., and Frank Scott. 1982. "The Income Tax and Nonwage Compensation." *Review of Economics and Statistics* 64(May): 211–219.

Luzadis, Rebecca, and Olivia Mitchell. 1991. "Explaining Pension Dynamics." *Journal of Human Resources* 26(Fall): 679–703.

Lynch, Lisa. 1992. "Private Sector Training and the Earnings of Young Workers." *American Economic Review* 82(March): 299–312.

Miner, John B., and Donald P. Crane. 1995. *Human Resource Management: The Strategic Perspective.* New York: HarperColllins.

Mischel, W., Y. Shoda, and M.L. Rodriguez. 1989. "Delay of Gratification in Children." *Science* 244: 933–938.

Mitchell, Daniel J.B., David Lewin, and Edward E. Lawler III. 1990. "Alternative Pay Systems, Firm Performance, and Productivity." In *Paying for Productivity*, Alan S. Blinder, ed. Washington, D.C.: The Brookings Institution, pp. 15–87.

Mitchell, Olivia, and Emily S. Andrews. 1981. "Scale Economies in Private Multi–Employer Pension Systems." *Industrial and Labor Relations Review* 34 (July): 522–530.

Mitchell, Olivia, and Sylvana Pozzebon. 1987. "Wages, Pensions and the Wage-Pension Tradeoff." Ithaca, New York: Cornell University. Mimeographed.

Mittelstaedt, H.F., and P.R. Regier. 1993. "The Market Response to Pension Plan Terminations." *Accounting Review* 68 (January): 1–27.

Montgomery, Edward, Kathryn Shaw, and Mary Ellen Benedict. 1992. "Pensions and Wages: An Hedonic Price Theory Approach." *International Economic Review* 33(February): 111–128.

Mutschler, Phyllis H. 1996. "Early Retirement Incentive Programs: Mechanisms for Encouraging Early Retirement." In *Handbook on Employment and the Elderly*, William H. Crown, ed. Westport, Connecticut: Greenwood Press.

Noe, Raymond A., John Hollenbeck, Patrick Wright, and Barry Gerhart. 1994. *Human Resource Management: Gaining a Competitive Advantage*. Burr Ridge, Illinois: Richard D. Irwin.

Office of Technology Assessment. U.S. Congress. 1990. *Worker Training: Competing in the International Economy*. OTA-ITE-457. Washington, D.C.: Government Printing Office.

Oi, Walter. 1983. "Heterogeneous Firms and the Organization of Production." *Economic Inquiry* 21(April): 147–171.

Papke, Leslie. 1995. "Participation in and Contributions to 401(k) Pension Plans." *Journal of Human Resources* 30(Spring): 311–325.

Papke, Leslie, Mitchell Petersen, and James M. Poterba. 1993. "Did 401(k)s Replace Other Employer-Provided Pensions?" In *New Issues in the Economics of Aging*, David Wise, ed. Chicago: University of Chicago Press.

Parsons, Donald O. 1992. "Transactions Costs in Pension Administration, Firm Size, and Pension Coverage." Columbus: Ohio State University. Mimeographed.

———. 1994. "Recent Trends in Pension Coverage Rates." In *Pension Coverage Issues for the '90s*, John Hinz, ed. Washington, D.C.: Government Printing Office.

Pesando, James, and Douglas Hyatt. 1992. "The Distribution of Investment Risk in Defined Benefit Pension Plans: A Re-Examination of the Evidence." Toronto: University of Toronto. Mimeographed.

Quinn, Joseph F., Richard V. Burkhauser, and Daniel A. Myers. 1990. *Passing the Torch: The Influence of Economic Incentives on Work and Retirement*. Kalamazoo, Michigan: W.E. Upjohn Institute for Employment Research.

Reagan, Patricia, and John A. Turner. 1994. "Youth, Taxes, and Pension Coverage." Columbus: Ohio State University. Mimeographed.

Rice, Robert G. 1966. "Skill, Earnings, and the Growth of Wage Supplements." *American Economic Review* 56(May): 583–593.

Rosen, Sherwin. 1985. "Implicit Contracts: A Survey." *Journal of Economic Literature* 23(September): 1144–1175.

Ross, Arthur. 1958. "Do We Have a New Industrial Feudalism?" *American Economic Review* 48(December): 903–920.

Salisbury, Dallas L. 1992. "Review of 'The Choice of Pension Plans in a Changing Regulatory Environment'." *Industrial and Labor Relations Review* 45(January): 387–388.

Samwick, Andrew A., and Jonathan Skinner. 1994. "How Will Defined Contribution Pensions Affect Retirement Income?" Hanover, N.H.: Dartmouth College. Mimeographed.

Schiller, Bradley, and Randall Weiss. 1979. "The Impact of Private Pension Plans on Firm Attachment." *Review of Economics and Statistics* 61(August): 369–380.

Schmitt, Ray, ed. 1993. *The Future of Pensions in the United States.* Pension Research Council. Philadelphia: University of Pennsylvania.

Silverman, Celia, and Paul Yakoboski. 1994. "Public and Private Pensions Today: An Overview of the System." In *Pension Funding and Taxation.* Dallas Salisbury and Nora Super Jones, eds. Washington, D.C: Employee Benefit Research Institute, pp. 7–42.

Simon, Herbert A. 1991. "Organizations and Markets." *Journal of Economic Perspectives* 5(Spring): 25–44.

Slichter, Sumner. 1921. *Turnover of Factor Labor.* New York: Appleton.

Statistics Canada. 1994. *Pension Plans in Canada.* Ottawa.

Stock, James H., and David A. Wise. 1990. "Pensions, the Option Value of Work, and Retirement." *Econometrica* 58(September): 1151–1180.

Turner, John A. 1993. *Pension Policy for a Mobile Labor Force.* Kalamazoo, Michigan: W.E. Upjohn Institute for Employment Research.

Turner, John A., and Daniel Beller. 1992. *Trends in Pensions.* Washington, D.C.: Government Printing Office.

Turner, John A., and Noriyasu Watanabe. 1995. *Private Pension Policies in Industrialized Countries: A Comparative Analysis.* Kalamazoo, Michigan: W.E. Upjohn Institute for Employment Research.

U.S. Chamber of Commerce. 1994. *Employee Benefits 1993.* Washington, D.C.: U.S. Chamber of Commerce.

U.S. Department of Labor. Bureau of Labor Statistics. 1996. *Employee Benefits in Medium and Large Private Establishments 1993.* Washington, D.C.: Government Printing Office.

U.S. Department of Labor. Pension and Welfare Benefits Administration. 1997. *Private Pension Plan Bulletin, Abstract of 1993 Form 5500 Annual Reports.* Washington, D.C.: Government Printing Office.

U.S. Senate, Subcommittee on Labor of the Committee on Labor and Public Welfare. 1976. *Legislative History of ERISA.* Washington, D.C.: 94th Congress (2nd Session).

Utgoff, Kathleen. 1991. "Towards a More Rational Pension Tax Policy: Equal Treatment for Small Business." *National Tax Journal* 64(September): 383–391.

Wachter, Michael L., and Randall D. Wright. 1990. "The Economics of Internal Labor Markets." *Industrial Relations* 29(Spring): 240–262.

Williamson, Samuel. 1994. "The Development of Industrial Pensions in the United States During the 20th Century." Oxford, Ohio: Miami University. Mimeographed.

Woodbury, Stephen A., and Douglas R. Bettinger. 1991. "The Decline of Fringe Benefit Coverage in the 1980s." In *Structural Changes in U.S. Labor Markets in the 1980s: Causes and Consequences*, Randall W. Eberts and Erica Groshen, eds. Armonk, New York: M.E. Sharpe.

Woodbury, Stephen A., and Wei-Jang Huang. 1991. *The Tax Treatment of Fringe Benefits*. Kalamazoo, Michigan: W.E. Upjohn Institute for Employment Research.

Author Index

Subject Index

ADEA. *See* Age Discrimination in
    Employment Act
Administration costs, of defined-benefit
    plans, 22
Age
    for peak benefits, 34
    pension impact on productivity and,
      54
    requirements and, 17
    See also Early retirement; Quit
      penalty; Retirement; Retirement
      incentives
Age Discrimination in Employment Act
    (ADEA, 1967), 33
Annuity, 3
    defined-benefit plans and, 17–18
Asymmetric information hiring model,
    40, 44–46

Backloading, 28, 50, 54, 60
Bonus. *See* Retirement incentives
Brookings Institution, 56
Budget deficits, taxation of pensions
    and, 21

Canada, defined-benefit plans on, 23n10
Cash or Deferred Arrangements
    (CODAs), 19, 22
"Cliff" rule of vesting, 17, 21
Cobb-Douglas model, 96, 99, 100, 101
    (table), 102
CODAs. *See* Cash or Deferred
    Arrangements (CODAs)
Compensation systems, 5
    alternative, 56
    pensions as deferred, 43–44
    productivity and, 55–57
    See also Firm-specific training model
Compustat Annual Industrial file, 93–94,
    97–99
Congress. *See* Federal policy

Constant nominal wage growth. *See*
    Wage growth
Contracts. *See* Employment contracts
Costs
    administrative, 68–69
    elasticity of pension, 55
    regulatory, 68
CPS. *See* Current Population Survey
Current Population Survey (CPS, 1991),
    73
    data from, 75–77
    estimates from, 78–83

Deferred compensation, 43–44, 47
Deficit Reduction Act (1984), 20
Defined-benefit plans
    administrative costs of, 22, 68
    Canada, 23n10
    career incentives of, 50–51, 109
    decline in coverage and, 15, 63–70
    discharge of workers and, 44, 47
    early retirement and, 6, 17
    eligibility age and, 29–33
    ERISA and, 21, 52n7
    federal policies and, 112
    firm productivity and, 94
    future of, 113
    as incentives, 33–36
    inflation risk of, 18
    large employers and, 18
    lump sum benefits and, 18
    nonportability of, 4
    primary coverage, by firm size, 66
    productivity and, 4, 5, 7
    quit penalties and, 25–27
    regulation of, 68
    retirement incentives of, 4, 33–36
    separation penalties and, 62
    training, productivity, and, 63
    turnover and, 60
    See also Incentive model of pensions
      and training; Productivity

About the Institute

The W.E. Upjohn Institute for Employment Research is a nonprofit research organization devoted to finding and promoting solutions to employment-related problems at the national, state, and local levels. It is an activity of the W.E. Upjohn Unemployment Trustee Corporation, which was established in 1932 to administer a fund set aside by the late Dr. W.E. Upjohn, founder of The Upjohn Company, to seek ways to counteract the loss of employment income during economic downturns.

The Institute is funded largely by income from the W.E. Upjohn Unemployment Trust, supplemented by outside grants, contracts, and sales of publications. Activities of the Institute comprise the following elements: 1) a research program conducted by a resident staff of professional social scientists; 2) a competitive grant program, which expands and complements the internal research program by providing financial support to researchers outside the Institute; 3) a publications program, which provides the major vehicle for disseminating the research of staff and grantees, as well as other selected works in the field; and 4) an Employment Management Services division, which manages most of the publicly funded employment and training programs in the local area.

The broad objectives of the Institute's research, grant, and publication programs are to 1) promote scholarship and experimentation on issues of public and private employment and unemployment policy, and 2) make knowledge and scholarship relevant and useful to policymakers in their pursuit of solutions to employment and unemployment problems.

Current areas of concentration for these programs include causes, consequences, and measures to alleviate unemployment; social insurance and income maintenance programs; compensation; workforce quality; work arrangements; family labor issues; labor-management relations; and regional economic development and local labor markets.